DON KING CAME CALLING

by

David C. Garland

CHAPTER ONE

The telephone call came during the early part of March of 1995 and was completely unexpected. I was very happy and looking forward with confidence to the future in my well-established position as Vice President for Corporate Development with CNN International, a burgeoning worldwide American television news network. At aged sixty years and six months I felt assured that I would remain with the same company until my retirement in four and a half years' time. My nine and a half years with the company had been both challenging and satisfying because I was doing exactly (maybe not "exactly" because, to be truthful, sitting down and writing novels was a long held dream) what I wanted in a business that was never less than exciting as it developed into a world-wide 24 hours a day, news phenomenon.

'David Garland?'

The voice on the line had a strong American accent flavoured with hints of Spanish origins.

'Yes.'

'My name is Hector Elizalde. I am a Vice President with Don King Productions based in Fort Lauderdale, Florida. Can I get right to the point?'

The mere mention of the name Don King suggested it would be wise to get right to the point without the slightest hint of hesitation.

'Please, be my guest, get right to the point!'

An amused, understanding, chuckle from Hector preceded his point.

'Don is looking for a person with sales experience in international television for the position of Director of International Sales. You have been recommended. I wonder whether you might be interested in meeting me to discuss the appointment?'

'Did you say your name is Hector?'

'Yes, Hector Elizalde.'

'Are you in Florida now?'

'No, I am at London Airport in transit to Warsaw. I'll be there for five days then back to London. If you are interested we can meet when I return.'

'So, I have a few days to think about this, correct?'

'Yes, think about it and I will call you when I get back to London in five days' time.'

'Okay, I will do that Hector.'

'Thank you David.'

Now why would I want to join Don King's company in sunny Florida when I had a perfectly good job in cold, rainy London? Silly question. The next day at the office there are rumours of a pending take-over. A huge American conglomerate, Time Warner, has made an audacious bid for the company. But, if it happens, nobody needs to worry insists sole-owner Ted Turner in a closed circuit television address to the staff; if the take-over goes through everybody's job will be safe he assures us, accompanied by a smile. So, feeling assured, we settled confidently back into our jobs safe in the knowledge that Ted Turner, the man whose innovative brain first spawned the idea of 24-hours-a-day television news, has told us unequivocally that no one was about to lose their job.

While awaiting the return of Hector Elizalde I got to thinking about my life and the jobs I have had since leaving school and how those jobs have led to my thinking about agreeing to meet a man with a Spanish name and a Spanish/American accent to talk about going to work in Florida, USA, for the world's most famous (or should that be infamous?) boxing promoter, the larger-than-life, wire-haired wonder, Don King.

It has been quite a journey.

CHAPTER TWO
EVACUATION
1939-1945

From the very first day I was born, my life has been a furious whirlwind of constant change, from poverty to more poverty, from town to town, from house to house and from problem to problem. It seemed at the time there was no escape from the noose that hangs around the neck of those unfortunates who are born impoverished and, apparently, forever doomed to remain so until something inexplicable happens that causes a revolution in the multi-thousand year mix of genes, thereby displacing the apathy born of poverty and replacing it with the determination that loosens the penurious knot, tosses it roughly aside and consequently provides the energy and stimulus to make something of one's life.

My father was descended from stock that originated in Deptford, a borough in south-east London, where he was born in 1899. My mother's origins were to be found at Worksop, a small town located in the Midlands of England.

How they came to meet and marry is a complete mystery and something that, strangely, I never bothered to ask them when they were alive. In retrospect I guess surviving was the one and only consideration and questions such as, "Where did you meet?" were deemed as irrelevant when compared to the everyday task of putting food on the table and, therefore, mundane questions were simply deemed unworthy of being addressed.

April 22, 1935. I was born at Downham, Bromley, Kent, a sprawling unlovely suburb of mainly council houses on the fringe of south London, the youngest of five children to Alfred and Eliza Garland. Growing up with one sister and three brothers in a tiny council house left few lasting memories. One memory however is etched, literally and indelibly, upon my skull. It was the result of an accident with the tin bath that was used for our weekly immersion in warm, soapy water; the Friday night bath. When the tin bath was not being used it was hung from a hook on the wooden fence in our back garden. I was about two years old and remember reaching for the tin bath, for no other reason than childish curiosity, when it fell and bounced to the ground, but not before ricocheting off the left hand side of my cranium. Mother came running. Blood was flowing and strips of torn shirt material were hastily produced to staunch the crimson tide flowing down my face. I still have the scar that I bear with much sadness. It is a constant reminder of my early beginnings. It is also a reminder of my first skirmish with danger from which I emerged wounded and bereft of hair for life in the particular spot where the tin bath struck.

My father was a wireworker at the Braby engineering works ten miles due north of Downham at Deptford in south east London, which meant he made wire safety cages that were placed around all sorts of dangerous machines in factories throughout Britain. Dad had irreparable damage to an index fingernail that was several layers thick, permanently blackened and irretrievably crumpled. Ironically I think he crushed the nail when making a safety cage for somebody's dangerous machine. My Dad's machine, I assume, couldn't have had a safety cage otherwise he wouldn't have suffered that crushed fingernail!

How he got to and from work each day I cannot imagine or recall. He probably boarded a succession of buses and trams armed with his early-morning worker's travel ticket. He never seemed to grumble about his journey or the arduous work but then you wouldn't if by comparison, at the tender age of eighteen, you harboured the life-changing experience of standing and fighting knee deep in mud in the stinking trenches of Flanders during the Great War; the one that was supposed to mark the end of future wars. He enrolled in the Royal West Kent Regiment and was proud to serve his country, volunteering at the tender age of seventeen. I shudder to think how today's youth would react to being embroiled in similar circumstances.

The Second World War was declared on September 3, 1939. Dad was forty years old when he was called-up once again for the army. He was enlisted into the Royal Artillery, leaving my mother with five children under the age of twelve. Vera was the eldest, followed in age by brothers Stanley, Alfred (known as Fred), Raymond and finally me, Dennis, the baby of the pack. Dad must have become sex-regimented as a result of his military service because there was a strict two years gap between all five siblings!

I can remember clearly the day my father left, scrubbed and tidied up, for re-enlistment in the army. My mother cried uncontrollably, Vera, Stanley, Alfred, Raymond and I, we also cried. We knew dad was going off to war and thought we would never see him again. He looked like Gary Cooper in his freshly pressed suit, clean white shirt, polished black shoes and wearing a left-over regimental tie from the Great War around his neck. His curly, dark hair was brushed back in the style of the day and his face, usually covered with stubble from two or three day's ignored growth, was as smooth as a new button and he smelled of strong carbolic soap, a smell I loved and which still reminds me to this day of my father. He looked around and smiled briefly as he marched up the road carrying a little dark-brown cardboard suitcase. He waved cheerfully as he was joined by other men who had also been called to serve King and country. By the time he reached the end of the long road where we lived there were ten males of varying ages, all marching in step, making their way to the bus that would take them to the recruiting centre in Lewisham, two miles into London proper.

My father was gone and the future suddenly appeared scary, lonely and very uncertain.

I'm not sure when it was decided the Garland family would move from the council house in Downham and evacuate to the comparative safety of Mansfield, a small market town in Nottinghamshire. My mother was born in Worksop, another market town twelve miles to the north-east. She had remnants of her family still living there and I suppose there must have been a family conference at which it was decided the move was prudent since it would avoid the bombs that were beginning to fall nightly on London. Mothers and children from all over London were being evacuated for the same reason so our family's move represented only a small portion of a very large, government-inspired, exodus to the country. Our family's exodus was to last five years and would act, I believe with the benefit of hindsight, as one of the reasons for enabling all five siblings to rise out of degrading poverty to varying levels of comfort.

I didn't know it at the time, after all I was only four years old, but Mansfield was a child's fantasy town surrounded as it was by the leafy glades of Sherwood Forest, home to Robin Hood, his Merry Men and Major Oak. Apparently Robin poached the King's deer in the royal hunting forest of Sherwood and unwary travellers moving through the forest provided rich pickings for the wily outlaw and his band. I would later be informed that the hollow trunk of the mighty Major Oak is said to have hidden Robin and his band of outlaws from the clutches of the Sheriff of Nottingham's men. At aged four years any story, no matter how bizarre, is totally believable!

During the next five years, while war raged throughout the world, my life and the lives of my sister and three brothers would change immeasurably and so would our London accents. If only a latter day Robin Hood had only been around to rob the rich and give to the poor, our fatherless family would have been grateful recipients of his largesse.

Our first "home" was supposed to have been a temporary refuge while something more permanent was found. It was called Westfield Folk House and my only recollection of its outward appearance is of a long drive leading to an imposing, dark-grey house. It had a gatehouse at the start of the drive where it joined the road. In the gate house was a storeroom that intrigued me because I often saw strange objects being taken inside while other equally strange objects were constantly being brought out. A man, dressed like a chauffeur, used to stand guard at the gatehouse as if he were a sergeant-major in the army. I would hide behind a tree nervously spying on the man while being totally engrossed with the goings-on but petrified in case I was seen and apprehended. To this day I never found out what went in and out of the gate-house but it still gives me the shivers when I think of the mysterious goings-on and the mysterious military-looking man in the chauffeur's outfit.

I wonder how many people have sat down and looked deeply into their young lives and then come to realise how many questions there are to be raised and, as a consequence, how many of those questions still remain unanswered? My oldest sibling Vera, only 12 at the time, was not living with us at Folk House and neither was Stanley, my oldest brother who was then ten years old. Why? Hmmm…..I know Vera was a live-in maid at a farm at Blidworth, a five-mile bus ride due south of Mansfield. I used to go to see her with my brothers, Alfred and Raymond and, strange to recall, we used to buy large lumps of horse meat from a butcher's shop in Mansfield and take it every Saturday to the farm where Vera would greet us dressed in the white and blue uniform of a house maid. What was done with the horse meat is another of those mysteries that puzzle me to this day and why was my young sister working as a house maid at such a tender age? She used to look so pretty, if prim and proper, in that blue and white uniform. And yet, sadly, she seemed to have grown distant from the family.

Notwithstanding my questions, I used to relish the opportunity to sneak into the farm's kitchen where a huge, cream coloured refrigerator was filled with fresh milk, freshly churned butter and jugs of cream as thick as custard. To a trio of hungry boys the visit to the farm was a weekly dream come true after the close-to-starvation diet we endured as a result of food rationing. Carrying huge slabs of butter home to Mum was a task I still recall with utmost joy since real butter had almost disappeared from our meal table to be replaced by insipid, tasteless government-introduced margarine.

Deep in the heart of Sherwood Forest was an army camp surrounded by a ten-foot high barbed wire fence. I used to go there with my mother and stand by the wire and wait until a certain soldier appeared who then threw huge loaves of freshly-baked bread over the fence. My mother must have practised her catching skills because I cannot recall her ever dropping one of those precious loaves, or perhaps it was an acquired skill that was honed by experience! This incident, however, raised another question in my immature mind. Why would a soldier throw loaves to my mother over the perimeter fence of his camp? Another hmmm that caused me many more hmmmmms......the answer would reveal itself in the not too distant future.

Westfield Folk House was great fun for the remaining three Garland boys since there were large, green areas in which to play, swings to swing upon, fences to jump over and not too many interfering adults to restrain us. Stanley was living on the other side of Mansfield in a large house owned by a spinster named Miss Manners. The house was much bigger than Folk House and unbelievably, to my inexperienced eyes, it contained a large outdoor swimming pool! Before getting carried away let me explain that the swimming pool was devoid of water for swimming but, instead, contained stagnant, evil smelling rain-water and the only creatures swimming were rather sad looking toads and frogs. Nevertheless, my eldest brother Stanley was living in a house with a swimming pool. To a young lad from the wrong side of the tracks this was the height of luxury since, before that time, I had no idea that people actually lived in houses that were not only detached from each other but also had their own swimming pools!

Notwithstanding the fact the pool was often knee deep in fetid, stagnant water we used to have a great time lobbing in lumps of mud while dangling our skinny legs over the concrete edge around the deep end. The poor frogs and toads must have been in a constant state of concussion during our visits to big brother Stanley's temporary home.

Back at Westfield Folk House there was a weekly gathering of cubs and boy scouts in a large shed to the side of the house. Kids from the local neighbourhood would arrive speaking in accents we struggled to understand while they, in turn, thought our accents posh which was daft in the extreme because we spoke in the south of the River Thames equivalent of the East End London cockney. The same shed was used on occasion by the local whist-drive club and this helped mother to become closely involved with the local female populace; her original Midlands accent, tempered by years of living in South London, was quickly revived, albeit unconsciously, as a result of mixing with her contemporaries. She appeared comfortable and at ease with herself being among those with whom she felt a bond.

I have no idea where the money came from to feed and clothe us since dad was in the army on minimal army pay and mum didn't work. I suppose there must have been allowances paid by the government to the families of servicemen in an amount that reflected the number of children in the family. Who knows, but how else did we survive?

One day we three brothers were playing on swings that were situated adjacent to a low fence at the boundary of Folk House and the house next door. Still being too young to join in the more extreme variations of swinging, I watched entranced as Alfred and Raymond stood on the wooden seat of the swing and worked gradually up to a height that was roughly parallel with the ground. As the swing descended they would leap off and attempt to land on the other side of the fence, to the next door garden. On one tragic occasion Raymond mistimed his leap and landed with his right leg impaled on one of the wooden fence struts. The leg was ripped open to the bone although, strangely, little blood flowed. He was rushed to hospital and several stitches were inserted before plaster of Paris was poured around his badly fractured leg. He must have been in agony because anaesthetics were in their infancy at the time and were certainly not available to the general public with the war in full flow. Our poor mum must have been driven to distraction, never knowing what awful circumstances her sons would become involved in next.

I slept in the same room as my mother. Alfred and Raymond were lucky -- they had a separate room where they would lie awake and discuss the affairs of the day until sleep brought a halt to their reminiscences. My single bed, however, was shunted into the far corner of the room with mum's double bed taking pride of place near one of the room's two windows that overlooked the shingle drive that led to the house.

During the course of one night, I cannot recall how old I was at the time, I clearly heard a man's voice from the area where my mother's bed was positioned. I was so excited by the thought that my father had returned from the war. The rest of the night was spent dreaming about dad. Imagine my disappointment upon waking the next morning to find mum alone. I told her about the man's voice that I had so clearly heard, thinking it was my father. She told me I must have been dreaming and said there had been no man's voice. Now, years later, I know why those loaves of bread were thrown over the fence at the army camp in Sherwood Forest! The voice I heard, I now have no doubt, was that of the kind soldier with the unerring aim. In the company of hundreds, thousands perhaps, of women left behind while their husbands went to war, I believe my mother took a lover to counter the painful loneliness that descends like a depressing cloak in the wake of enforced parting. It is very likely that my father also did the same, stranded as he was miles from home and with his life on a knife edge every time squadrons of heavily laden German bombers appeared on the horizon, droning ominously, over southern England.

It was something that was never referred to after the war was over.

I cannot recall how long we stayed at Westfield Folk House or why we left it but I do recall being shunted with Mum, Fred and Ray to the other side of Mansfield where we settled into an end of terrace house in Clarkson Street which we shared with a grouchy, ageing couple. We were cramped into two tiny rooms with minimalist furniture; perhaps, on reflection, we were the origins of the futuristic style of minimalist living without being aware of it!

It was a long way short of the space we had become accustomed to at Westfield Folk House. In order to gain access to drinking water, we had to pass countless times a day through the old folk's living room, bulbous glass jug in hand, to the kitchen where water was on hand via a rusting, leaking tap. Raymond, now recovered from the accident to his leg, was back to his old practical-joking self. One afternoon, when the old man was snoozing on the couch in his living room, Ray went to refill the water jug. After filling it to the brim he tiptoed back and, for a reason he was later unable to explain, deliberately spilt water onto the head of the sleeping man. All Hell broke loose and a week later we were ejected from the house and relocated further down the street at number seventeen. It was here, at the new house, that we acquired our first dog.

Having heard petrified squealing from the vicinity of next door's back yard, Fred and I looked over the adjoining fence to see five or six puppies being deliberately drowned in a rainwater barrel. A woman was picking them up from a basket, one by one, and plunging the tiny, new born, puppies into the stagnant rain water. I cried aloud upon seeing the carnage and pleaded for her to stop. My voice, strengthened by the horror I was witnessing, was resonant enough to cause the woman to stop and look around for the source of the intervention. She wagged a dripping-wet finger at the two of us and told us to mind our own business. The final puppy was about to be thrust under the water when Fred yelled in repulsion at the sight before his eyes, his voice unconsciously reverting to his fast disappearing south London accent.

'Stop, we'll 'ave that one!'

The woman, hearing the strange accent, looked around again and stopped her plunging. She looked at the two appealing faces peering over the fence, looked down at the handful of puppy in her hand and began walking towards us.

'You part of the new folks?' she asked suspiciously upon reaching and looking over the fence.

Two heads nodded in unison.

She looked once more at the squirming sausage wriggling in her podgy hand, emitted an understanding sigh and handed it over to Fred.

'Look after the little bugger and mek sure it don't come into our yard when it puts meat on!'

Fred looked at the woman and smiled as broadly as if he'd been handed Adolf Hitler's head on a platter.

'Thank you,' he said, 'Thank you very much.'

The tiny bundle, sensing salvation, gave a delighted squeal. Fred smiled, I smiled, and even the dog-dunking woman relented and gave the slightest hint of a smile.

'Now, away wit pair of you before I change me mind.' she said.

I cannot remember what Mum had to say when we presented her with our newly acquired bundle but, suffice to say, the dog (which we named Gyp) became part of the family. She blossomed into a large Alsatian cross breed who was much loved and, to a certain extent, helped soften the blow which was falling upon a family that was slowly disintegrating as the months inexorably turned into years.

Stanley, now aged eleven, gained a place at posh Brunts Grammar School located in the north-east of Mansfield. This was quite an achievement since he had to sit and pass several examinations to a very high standard. His success was the first indication that the millennium-long mix of genes was producing its first positive result. Entry to Brunts was the ultimate objective of parents living in Mansfield as their children reached the end of a six-year education at primary schools, and I was puffed up with pride that my big brother had achieved the objective in spite of all the disadvantages and obstacles he had so admirably surmounted. Stanley, as a consequence, became my first hero!

Alfred and Raymond attended St. Peter's C of E Primary School about two miles from where we were living. This meant a long walk to and from school each day without adult company, without a rain coat, hand-in-hand, no matter what the weather. As I strain to recall those days

I associate my years in Mansfield with rain, dark looming clouds, icicles and deep, deep snow; which is a great pity because I am sure there must have been periods of the year when the sun shone just as brightly as during those summers spent in south London when the world was at peace and I had my father to tuck me into bed at night.

I, meanwhile, was about to start school for the first time. So, instead of two of the Garland boys trudging through the streets of Mansfield heading for another day's schooling, I joined my brothers and left my mother alone at home to do what mothers do in times of war.

The football boots I wore to school that first morning were minus the long, leather studs that were usually hammered into the soles to give the wearer a grip on grass and mud. I was thankful for this because it made it easier for me to walk the two miles of unyielding stone pavements that faced me in the morning and upon the return in the late afternoon. The problem was the boots were too big and my feet slopped around in them despite of wearing two pairs of hand-me-down, darned socks. Consequently my feet were rubbed so sore that I had to report to the school nurse after the first morning's trudge landed me at the school's entrance.

'Why are your feet so sore,' the nurse asked sympathetically.

'It's the football boots,' was all I could reply. After all, this was my first day at school and everything was so strange and there were too many things happening for my five year old brain to absorb.

'Football boots?' replied the bewildered nurse. 'Why are you wearing football boots?'

'I don't have any shoes, so I wear my brother's old football boots. They are too small for him but too big for me!'

The nurse carried on tending to my sore feet by massaging them with a shiny translucent gel called Vaseline. She then bandaged the areas around my feet where the soreness was most apparent. The bloodied socks were set aside for washing and, from somewhere, she produced worn but clean socks that she gently eased over my feet that now looked twice their size, wrapped as they were in layer after layer of bandage. The football boots now fitted and my feet were snug as a baby in swaddling clothes.

Thanking the nurse I made my way to my allotted classroom where the first lesson of the day was already under way. My entry caused gales of laughter to erupt from the assembled pupils.

'Hey look, the new boy's wearing football boots. He's ready for play time,' cried someone in disbelief.

'Look how big they are,' yelled somebody else, mouth agape.

The teacher, whom I later learned was named Miss Carter, stilled the class into silence with a sharp rap of a thin cane on the top of her desk.

'Silence,' she ordered while simultaneously staring at my huge leather-clad feet. The sight was even more grotesque now because the loose ends of the bandages were waving and flapping every time I took a step towards the teacher.

'Why are you wearing those things?' she gasped, still unable to believe what had walked into her classroom.

'They're all I 'ave Miss', I stammered, my London accent now adding a new reason for an increasing buzz of whispered conversation among my fellow pupils. A look of compassion crossed Miss Carter's face and I swear I saw the glint of tears appearing in the corners of her eyes.

'What is your name child?' she asked quietly while once more ominously lifting the cane that immediately had the effect of hushing the class.

I continued staring at the ground in red-faced embarrassment.

'Dennis Garland Miss.'

Miss Carter laid a gentle hand on my shoulder and addressed the class.

'Did you hear his name children?' she said to complete silence while picking up a piece of note paper lying on her desk. She read its contents before readdressing the class.

'Dennis is from London and is here with his mother, sister and three brothers to escape the bombs that are falling on London every night. I want you all to be very kind to him and help him settle into school.'

She paused, surveying the sombre, under impressed class.

'Dennis please go and sit next to Percy, over there in the front row.' Miss Carter indicated towards an empty seat behind a desk with two seating positions. 'Percy I want you to help Dennis settle in. Can you do that for me?'

Poor Percy Dakin didn't know where to look -- at me, at Miss Carter or at his fellow pupils, so instead he stared blankly at his desk top. His mild complexion, topped by flaming ginger hair, turned the colour of beetroot while his mouth remained steadfastly shut.

'Percy, did you hear what I said?' Miss Carter moved towards the seated unfortunate chosen to partner me, the new boy wearing outsize football boots.

'Yes Miss,' he eventually managed to mumble. 'I have to help him settle in.'

'Thank you Percy but it is not "him" but rather "Dennis." Do you understand?'

Percy nodded his head quickly while his mouth froze into a grimace. He glared menacingly at me as I let down the spring-loaded, dark oak seat next to his and plonked myself down, my football boots making horrible scraping noises as I squirmed into the narrow space between the seat and the base of the desk top.

'Now children let's settle down. In this morning's lesson we will learn the alphabet. Who knows how many letters there are in the alphabet?'

The rest of the lesson was too horrible to relate. I didn't know where to look, what to do and I failed to answer any questions correctly. I wished the world would end there and then but of course it didn't and, consequently, the first day's playground break beckoned and I was horrified when I experienced what lay in store for me next.

The playground at the rear of the school was typical of the day. Grey, uneven asphalt covered the entire area that was about the size of half a football pitch. Once-white lines were painted on its surface denoting the positions where individual classes lined up before marching, crocodile-fashion, into the classrooms. The area was surrounded by a six-foot high red brick wall on which were painted goal posts and cricket wickets. The forbidding school building, dating from the late nineteenth century, rose tomb-like, three stories above the playground and was capped by a depressing looking roof comprised of dark blue-grey slates. It was drizzling and a cold breeze swirled around the playground forcing the pupils into huddled groups as a way of gaining a mite of warmth and succour.

I stood alone. Percy had abandoned me the moment the double-door to the playground was flung open and he headed without a backward glance towards his long term friends. At that singular moment I experienced a sense of loneliness that was purely physical. By that I mean it hurt, badly. The noise of the children around me suddenly quietened as if someone had turned down the sound on a radio and all I could see were silent children running to and fro, their mouths moving, their voices mute. The playtime's allocated fifteen minutes lasted for what seemed an hour as I stood, back against the wall of the school, forlorn and friendless. That was until I saw the familiar figures of my brothers Alfred and Raymond appearing in the near distance. Tears running down my face trickled through the grime of the morning and left pink rivulets as a reminder of my sadness.

'Don't cry,' said Alfred taking my grubby, shaking, hand in his. 'You'll soon make friends. The first day is always the worst.'

Alfred and Raymond stared long and hard at my football boots; the flapping white bandages now wet, tangled and streaked with mud and other suspicious looking grunge.

'Your poor little bugger,' said Raymond empathetically; this from a seven year old whose experience of life was only two years in advance of mine.

CHAPTER THREE
BACK TO THE SMOKE
1945-1950

The family remained in Mansfield until May 7, 1945. This was the date when the exhausted German armies finally surrendered to the rampaging Allied forces. It signalled the end of our enforced exile and the start of a safe return to London now that squadron upon squadron of German bombers no longer appeared on the horizon each night dropping incendiary and high explosive bombs, and now that unmanned V1 and V2 rockets no longer streaked through the skies of southern England to wreak death and destruction on our beloved, abandoned, London and its indefatigable inhabitants.

The four years and several months spent in Mansfield hold no treasured or lasting memories for me. They were long years of depressing deprivation, of freezing cold winters, of a family driven apart through no fault of their own, of not knowing whether we would all become subject to rule by Adolf Hitler's Nazi's or whether the valiant

Allied forces would finally prevail. Those experiences, those thoughts, those deprivations, those awful years, left their individual mark on each and every one of us. But there was much more to come.

Our council-owned house at Downham, the one we left in September of 1939, was no longer available to us. A new family, forced to quit their home destroyed in the Blitz nearer the epicentre of the bombing of London, was now living in the house where the tin bath had fallen on my head. Also not available to us upon our return was our furniture and belongings that were left behind after our hasty exodus to the midlands of England. To this day I have no idea what happened to those everyday things that were part and parcel of our past lives, but does it really matter? With the passage of time questions such as these in the aftermath of a horrific war were considered an irrelevance. The only objective upon our return to an almost totally destroyed inner London was that of maintaining a day-to-day survival.

We did bring something with us however, something we would quickly attempt to discard because it set us apart from the people we began to mix with upon our return; the alien accent we had picked up and adopted in everyday speech in those years away from our roots. At the age of nine there is a serious integration disadvantage with new-found contemporaries if you are supposedly different. So, work on regaining our London accents began the moment we all alighted from the train as it ground, swathed in acrid-smelling steam, to a panting, wheezing halt in London's Paddington station.

'This is it boys,' said mother. 'We're back in London.'

Mum was almost correct, save for the fact that our sister Vera, now closing on eighteen years of age, was still working at the farm in Blidworth where we brothers had experienced some of the good things that life has to offer. Gyp, our dog, now a two year old tearaway who refused to obey any order which did not fit in with her current objectives, was the only addition to the family which had left London back in September of 1939.

With battered suitcases, plus a dog on a lead of discarded rope being dragged along with great difficulty in our wake, we took another train from London's Charing

Cross station which, twenty-five minutes later, dropped us off at Greenwich, a suburb in south London close to where our father had worked so assiduously before the outbreak of war. But where were we to live? The answer arrived quickly, accompanied by a general feeling of deep gloom and depression.

The school had been commandeered by the government as temporary shelter for returning evacuees. It was sited at the foot of a hill in Greenwich Park, part of the suburb of the same name in south London, bounded on one side by the River Thames. Entire families were herded into the school building, provided with very basic bedding and allocated space in one of the various rooms in the school. Space for our family was in the large school assembly hall. There was barely enough room to turn over as the six of us, Mother, Stanley, Alfred, Raymond, me and our dog Gyp, bedded down for our first night back in the "Smoke" (the cockney's sardonic name for London at the time, so called because of the lung burning, green-yellow sulphur dioxide fog that descended like a funeral shroud each winter and killed thousands of people, mainly the those suffering from chest problems, the very old and the very young). Mother dangled spare blankets over thin ropes to act as dividers and to give some privacy to and from the adjacent families.

'This isn't too bad is it?' Mum said in a brave effort to raise our down-in-the-dumps spirits, 'It won't be for too long. As soon as dad gets out of the army we'll be given a house and we can all be back together again.'

Stanley at sixteen, the oldest of the four boys, having become used to his own bedroom, bathroom and toilet at the posh home of Miss Manners, looked aghast at the sights surrounding us and placed his head woefully into his two hands.

'Mum, this is terrible,' he answered. 'We should have stayed in Mansfield.'

I didn't find the temporary accommodation that demoralising, basic though it was, but access to washing and toilet facilities was, on occasion, grossly inadequate and often embarrassing. For how many weeks we endured these conditions I cannot recall. What I do remember with perfect clarity is the first house that was allocated to our family by the housing department based at the local council offices. We were assigned a house despite the fact that dad was still in the army but expected to be "demobbed" and on his way home at any time. In my simple mind the reason for the early allocation was straightforward. Gyp, our lovely, now fully grown dog, was keeping everyone awake at night with her continuous barking whenever someone shifted position in their uncomfortable beds. I have never seen so many people so pleased to see the back of a family and its dog as were those unfortunates left behind.

Number 17, Floyd Road, Charlton, a south London suburb immediately adjacent to Greenwich, was a Victorian terraced house comprising a basement and three upper floors. The basement and ground floors were already occupied by a family when we moved in. We had use of the second and third floors. Once again my memory is blank as to where we acquired furniture for the house. Did the local council also provide furniture, in addition to the house? Or was there a charity that assisted evacuees returning to London after the war with such basics as beds, bedding, kitchen table and chairs, cutlery, cooking utensils, towels, etcetera? Questions, questions! In setting out to write this autobiography I had not anticipated or envisaged that I would be faced with the fact that there is so much of my early life that includes questions that may never be answered.

September 1945 and our dad arrived home from the army. He knocked on the door to our new home nattily dressed in a dark blue, pin-striped suit, white shirt, grey trilby hat, regimental tie, navy blue socks and black, shiny shoes; standard issue, with some personal choice thrown in, to all military personnel upon demobilisation from His Majesty's forces. He stood there at the door arms stretched out wide, his stuffed beige coloured kitbag resting on the concrete path, grinning from ear to ear. He looked so handsome, so smart that I cried, as did Raymond, Alfred and even our eldest brother Stanley shed a few tears. Mum may have cried too but I was unable to see whether she did because dad hugged her so tightly that they became one person again. To ten-year-old me, dad was home and all our troubles were at an end!

The house was in a terrible state of disrepair, everything needed renovating and decorating. There was no electricity; evil smelling, poisonous sulphurous gas extracted from coal provided our lighting via wall-mounted brass outlets on which perched fragile gas mantles that immediately fell apart if inadvertently touched when being lit. The resulting light was a garish yellow hue which made everyone in the room appear as if they had a severe bout of advanced jaundice.

We hadn't realised how bad things were until the first winter -- that of 1945/1946 -- arrived. Dad was back at his old job with Braby's engineering works at Deptford and had saved enough to buy linoleum to cover the floor of the sitting room (or rather a room that was intended for sitting but was doubling up as a bedroom for Stanley). The wind whistled through the creaking house with such ferocity that it lifted dad's new linoleum off the floorboards so that it resembled a moving sea crested with gentle, flowing waves. And it was freezing cold. It inevitably cast my mind back to those awful, never-ending, winters in Mansfield. Luckily we had dad's old army overcoat to add to the two blankets laid over the double, iron-framed, bed where Raymond and I tried to grab a few hours of uninterrupted sleep. Never, previously or since, have I experienced such penetrating cold and we had little or nothing available to combat its debilitating effects.

The range in our tiny kitchen was the only place in the entire house where something approaching warmth was available. The range, made of cast iron, was polished periodically with black lead to make it shine. It stood in a chimney recess at the back of the kitchen. It was fuelled each day with either huge lumps of gleaming coal or logs, depending on fiscal circumstances; in other words, what our dad could afford! The blazing fire could be seen through grills on its front. Adjacent to this was a small oven the heat of which was uncontrollable. On its surface were two cast-iron, round lift-off plates where kettles eventually reached boiling point and where vegetables were over-boiled, for so long that green cabbages ended up a pasty translucent, tasteless, soggy mess. Chinese stir fry was still years away in the distant future!

Coal was delivered once a week by horse-drawn drays. It would be dumped in the road outside one's house whereupon the householder had to shovel it into an outside manhole which gave access to an underground cellar. It was a daily, scary, chore to venture into the depths of the pitch black cellar to fill a coal scuttle with sufficient fuel for the day's heating and cooking, a task that scared the daylights out of me, fearful as I was of rats, mice and things that go bump in the dark!

The yard at the back of the house backed onto a railway line where trains from London's main line stations at Charing Cross and Cannon Street would constantly clatter past on their way to or from Woolwich and points north to Dartford. Alfred's bedroom overlooked the yard.

One morning I went to wake him for school. His bed was covered in lumps of ceiling plaster while a coating of white dust blanketed everything in the room. Since the house was built the ceiling had been subject to the constant passage of clattering, earth shaking, trains and then, during the war years, by horrendous reverberations caused by high explosive bombs dropping in the same street.

Alfred remained blissfully asleep, unaware that, but for the grace of God, he could have been killed while he slept. The ceiling remained thereafter in a state of odious disrepair. Dad couldn't repair it and the workmen from Greenwich Borough Council were far too busy renovating bomb-damaged houses to have the time to fix a gaping hole in a nobody's ceiling.

At the bend in our road of crumbling terraced Victorian houses, where it swept downwards in an s-curve to join lower road, were the remains of a house destroyed by an incendiary bomb. We used to have a great time clambering over the mounds of rubble pretending we were soldiers. Later we cleared a large patch which we used as a head-tennis court. The football used for this activity was the heavy, leather version inside which was a rubber bladder that had to be pumped full of air. The one we were playing with had bounced hundreds of times on and off the crumbling concrete floors and brick walls. Consequently it was scuffed, scarred and embedded with pieces of sharp grit. Our filthy, bloodied, foreheads bore scars that were an undeniable testament to our commitment to the game. Nevertheless our heading skills improved with every game and helped foster a desire to play football at the very highest level.

Charlton Athletic Football Club, nicknamed "The Addicks" at the time, was the local First Division professional club. The first team played with varying degrees of success every other week at The Valley, a monster of a ground located at the end of the lower end of Floyd Road. Living so close to a major football club was pure bliss to a boy of ten whose experience of professional football was previously limited to probably three visits to Field Mill, the tiny football ground in Mansfield where the local side was humbled each week by teams from the wartime Third Division North. My allegiance to Mansfield disappeared in clouds of euphoria in the first Saturday I was taken by my brother Stanley to see Charlton play fellow-Londoners Arsenal.

I was one among a crowd of 70,000 and that day, standing on tiptoe behind the goal where England's, ginger-haired, goalkeeper, Sam Bartram, performed his daring, sky-diving heroics, I fell in love with Charlton Athletic and discarded, without the slightest hint of regret, the last remaining link with the town where I had spent those terrible war years; Mansfield in the county of Nottinghamshire.

Alan Starbuck was the star footballer of Floyd Road. If he had been around at the start of the new millennium he would have been on Chelsea's books earning £150,000 a week. A natural left footer, he could dribble cumbersome leather, mud-covered footballs past bewildered defenders with the ease of a steak knife slicing through a perfectly cooked fillet of beef. His left foot delivered blistering shots as if fired from the gun of a Sherman tank. Goalkeepers blanched and feigned distraction when they caught sight of him about to blast the ball in their direction. Not only was he a great footballer but he also had the looks of a Hollywood screen idol. Curly black hair, a slim figure honed to physical perfection, a way with the girls that had me thinking I would never land a female companion, bereft as I was of chat-up lines and, wonder of wonders, his father, mother and three male siblings ran the local greengrocery shop!

The excitement didn't stop there. He was the first person I had seen wearing the latest item of must-have clothing -- blue jeans! And what's more, he delivered his family's greengrocery throughout the surrounding district by means of a horse drawn cart! Would the excitement never end?

Alan used to take me with him on the cart and, once I'd overcome my fear of horses, I was allowed to take the reins and quickly learned to persuade the lazy, grumpy horse to pull the heavily laden cart to its next stop on the daily delivery route. Pretty young housewives emerging from row-upon-row of terraced council houses would fling open their front doors as Alan's voice was heard singing the praises of his onions and carrots. They would arrive, panting with excitement, to stand by the horse and cart just to catch sight of their blue-jean clad heartthrob weighing a sexy mix of fruit and vegetables. He wore a permanent smile on his rugged, Tony Curtis-like, features and knew, without any hint of bravado, that he was highly attractive to a host of young women.

I used to wonder why he took so long to dump the baskets of greengrocery inside the houses of those women who were, ostensibly, too weak to carry them. Before he entered the door of a household in the wake of a nervously tittering young thing he would turn to me, saucily wink a smoky-brown eye and give me a jaunty thumbs-up. The service he provided was obviously first-class because we never returned to his family's greengrocery shop with any unsold goods still on the cart.

Alan's younger brother Ernie was so different that he must have been sired by someone other than Alan's father. He was an absolute terror. When he appeared in the road all signs of activity among the younger elements stopped as if someone had pushed the pause button on a video player. The road cleared as if a dire warning had been posted about the return of the Great Plague. He would beat up anyone and everyone who displeased him. Fierce dogs would shamble around and by him, fear overtly displayed in their bloodshot eyes. Grown men would quiver and quake at his approach. But, for some inexplicable reason, he tolerated me. It wasn't because I was a really good footballer like his brother Alan or indeed like him in any way. It wasn't because of anything I was aware of, in fact there was nothing I could point to and say, 'That's the reason, that's why Ernie likes me.'

I wasn't about to displease Ernie by attempting to define the elusive reason for my good fortune so I carried on playing with him in the road, fooling around with him wherever and whenever he dictated and watched, nonplussed, as he berated others while I enjoyed the sanctuary of the benevolence he showered upon me.

Alan's eldest brother Joey suddenly appeared on the local scene. I had been living in Floyd Road for over a year now and spell-binding tales about Alan's big brother Joey were passed around our gang. He was reputed, alongside many other exciting back-of-the-hand whispered suggestions, to be an assassin in the SAS, a freedom fighter in Cuba, a sergeant in the French Foreign Legion and a fearless stunt man in Hollywood. The street was a hotbed of salacious gossip until the real reason for his sudden appearance was presciently revealed by his brother Ernie. He had been finally released from a lengthy spell in prison! Yes, Joey was a jail bird and an unwilling guest of His Majesty King George V1. A fallen hero who left the scruffy, war-torn kids living in Floyd Road with broken dreams and a realisation that fame is fleeting and invariably dependent on the most fragile of outrageous lies.

I was now ten years old and attending Sherington Road Primary School about a two mile walk from our house and I was being bullied. The boy who sat next to me would pinch and punch me constantly within and without the classroom. The reason? I think it was because I still had the remnants of a midlands accent and was good at most subjects including English, maths, history, geography, art and music. Being top in these subjects, while pleasing my parents, unfortunately made me, literally, a sitting target as I was assumed to be a teacher's pet.

Mum worried about me. She could sense something was wrong by translating the pained look on my face as I arrived home after school each evening.

'You're being bullied aren't you?' she stated unequivocally, defying me to say she was wrong in her assumption. 'Who is it? Tell me who it is and I will be up at that school and put a stop to it!'

I resisted divulging the name of my classmate until the bullying became so bad that I was making all sorts of lame excuses not to go to school. This clinched it for mother and she forced the name out of me by using the most pernicious of persuasion methods, one that never failed.

'All right,' she said. 'Unless you tell me his name you will get no more home-made apple pie – ever!'

Since Mum's apple pie was the best in the whole wide world, the name of my tormentor left my lips with the alacrity of a world champion 100 yard sprint champion scorching down the track propelled by a massive dose of steroids. The next day, during one of the morning lessons, the classroom door suddenly opened and my mother appeared dressed in her Sunday best. She walked up to Miss Doig, our form teacher, introduced herself and explained the reason for her visit. The culprit sitting next to me shifted uneasily in his seat and gave me a look of absolute shock and horror.

'You split on me.' His face was twisted into an ugly shape that revealed fear and loathing at the same time.

Miss Doig brought the two of us to the front of the class and rat face, my unspoken nickname for my tormentor, was made to apologise. We were "invited" to shake hands and then we set off back to our two-seater bench at the back of the class accompanied by a hum of whispered conversation emanating from the rest of the class.

Mother left, satisfied that the bully had been put in his place. Unfortunately, I was left to suffer, for the remaining year at Sherington Road Primary School, the slings and arrows of outrageous wrath from Rat Face and his close friends. I vowed, there and then, despite the threat of life-long deprivation of mother's apple pie that I would never again divulge the name of a tormentor but, instead, I would settle the matter personally. That was the day when I became a man.

These were the days of the 11-plus examination. Pupils were set examinations at the close of their years at primary school; examinations designed to determine the next appropriate step in the educational process. To my great delight and that of my family I passed the exam which meant I was selected for a grammar school education. The school in question was the one for which my parents had offered their prayers. Known as Roan Grammar School for Boys it sat proudly atop the peak of Maze Hill in Greenwich, about three miles from our home in Charlton. While familial delight was abroad at my success it was tempered with a large degree of financial anxiety. School uniform was a strict requirement at Roan Grammar and that meant buying the green jacket emblazoned with the school motif (a silver stag's head), grey trousers, a green and black striped tie, grey socks and brown shoes. On top of these basic items were shorts and singlets for the gymnasium, football boots, plimsolls and two or three books that were necessary adjuncts to my forthcoming education but, unfortunately, were not provided by the school. The cost of buying the package was equivalent to the wage my father received in a week! This was too much of a financial burden to bear so mother set out on a mission to buy second-hand. Her endeavours paid off but I ended up with a jacket that was far too big for me and frayed at the cuffs, a tie that had seen far better days, short grey trousers that required patching, darned socks and black, scuffed shoes that I polished ferociously with brown shoe polish in an effort to make them match the tan shoes worn by my new classmates. Because of the patched trousers I earned the nickname "Patchy" that was to stay with me to my utter chagrin during the five years at Roan Grammar. My parents must have been so proud to have a son who was wearing a grammar school uniform including a cap with a shiny metal badge in the shape of a stag's head. One drawback, however, manifested itself on the way to the new school on that very first morning. The local trams from Charlton to Maze Hill, Greenwich, numbers 36, 38 and 40, stopped at the end of the hill that was Church Road where it met Greenwich Road. I boarded the tram and went upstairs to be confronted by a gang of youngsters of about the same age as me. They were making their way to Charlton Central School, a few stops along the same route I was taking. They saw my bright green jacket and my matching green cap and immediately began berating me for being posh and going to a grammar school. They pulled and tugged at me and, to be very honest, I was terrified.

One against six are odds I still do not accept as being winnable. Therefore I was mightily relieved when the tram conductor intervened and put a stop to their rowdy behaviour. I was even more relieved when the six alighted from the tram at the Charlton Central stop -- albeit they stood on the pavement waving their fists at me as I slunk deeper into my seat and pretended not to notice them by using the clever trick of looking the other way! It was a humbling experience and clearly demonstrated the problems that can arise from being different to one's contemporaries.

But there would be many more such instances as I proceeded to try to better myself, while attempting to discard the tormenting shackles imposed by a short lifetime of poverty.

Alfred and Raymond had already sat and, sadly, failed their 11-plus examinations and were as a consequence assigned to the local boy's school, Charlton Central, where the accent was on vocational training. Alfred showed great aptitude at things electrical while Raymond appeared to be heading for a job in the council library; his head was never out of a book. Sister Vera, forever the traveller, had now left her position as a maid at the farm in Blidworth and was enrolled in the Royal Navy. Women in the Senior Service in those days were known as "Wrens", an acronym for Women's Royal Naval Service. I remember her coming home on leave once with a man friend who was also in the Navy. The most impressive thing about her friend, whose name I forget, was his fountain pen. It was a black, shiny De la Rue and, to my 12-year-old deprived eyes the pen was an amazing masterpiece. If only I had that beautiful pen to take to school perhaps my nick name "Patchy" would be forgotten amid the jealousy that would be engendered among my, fountain pen-less, contemporaries. However, it was not to be and I had to be content with my school-supplied, wooden pen with a nib that had to be constantly dipped into dark-blue, sticky ink which was deposited in a grey porcelain holder sunk in a round hole in the corner of my battered desk.

Vera ditched the naval pen man later and eventually married another sailor named Norman Edwards who was really nice -- he gave me one of his naval shirts as a present. It was white and very stiff, with short sleeves (although they were long on me) and a large oblong, navy-blue trimmed opening through which one thrust one's head. It was far too big but I felt so proud walking up and down Floyd Road and the local streets wearing the shirt while adopting the rolling gait of a sailor! Ernie Starbuck must have liked it because when he saw me wearing it for the first time he asked me to hand it over which I promptly did. Well, it was an order I couldn't refuse, if you see what I mean!

Meanwhile my eldest brother Stanley was already hard at work. He had joined Dad as an apprentice engineer at Braby's two years ago and appeared to be content and happy. There was, however an inescapable duty on the horizon; two year's obligatory National Service for each and every young man upon reaching eighteen years of age!

Stanley was called up in February of 1947 and, after basic training, was assigned to the Royal Horse Guards, one of the most elite regiments in the British army. He had left home, trepidation evident in his demeanour but now, on his first leave, he was transformed. Confidence was paramount in everything he did. Meticulously tidy, everything had its place. I was so proud of him; my big brother was the personification of everything I longed to be!

After a short leave he returned to barracks and within three weeks he and his fellow recruits were shipped off to a camp in West Berlin Germany where, two years after hostilities had ceased, chaos still reigned. Berlin was divided. The Allies occupied Berlin's western section. The USSR ruled with an iron fist in the eastern portion where a dividing wall was eventually erected by the Russians and their East German subordinates.

Letters from Stanley were opened with a mixture of excitement allied to concern as to his well-being. I was designated the answerer-in-chief, a task I enjoyed immensely due to my love of writing. Invariably he requested we send him packets of ground coffee which, as we discovered upon his return after demobilisation, was used as a form of currency to purchase all manner of things, including favours from German women!

Upon his return to civilian life he returned to his job at Braby's Engineering where dad was still employed making safety cages for dangerous machines.

Roan Grammar School was a revelation. All the teachers wore long, flowing black cloaks over their suits. At assembly each morning we sang the school hymn – I still remember most of the first verse.

Here's to old John Roan who lived and worked and died

In the mighty days of Cromwell of Milton and of Blake

He was born in days of passion, he was reared in days of pride

He gave himself to England and to Continents beside.

What can we give for our founder's sake?

Ourselves we give to England till John Roan shall wake.

After singing the school hymn we had prayers and then, horror piled upon horror, a piece of really drab, boring classical music that was played upon a scratchy gramophone by Mr. Trottman, the music master. We had to listen intently and absorb what was being played because during the next music lesson Trottman would ask us questions about the piece played and woe betide anyone if he didn't have the answers.

I remember one occasion when, before entering the music lesson, my closest pal Colin Collnet, an inveterate chewer of Wrigley's Spearmint gum, placed a large mouthful behind his ear, as was his wont, for safe keeping until the music lesson was over. Colin was asked a music question that he couldn't answer, so Trottman took him by the ear and began leading him to the front of the class to deal out admonition, which was usually a hearty whack of the cane. Halfway to his destination Mr. Trottman became aware of something sticking to his fingers. Drawing his hand away he saw an unbroken stretch of sticky, grey chewing gum forming a swaying bridge between his hand and Colin's ear. Trottman went ballistic. His eyes bulged like oversized cannon-balls, his face turned the colour of a ripe Victoria plum and the air turned blue as foreign-sounding expletives tumbled in a never ending torrent from his spluttering mouth. The entire class collapsed into bursts of uproarious laughter. Colin stood shaking like a lonely flag in a stiff breeze while desperately attempting to disengage the gum from his ear. The hubbub brought the headmaster running into the class together with other members of staff. Trottman remained apoplexic, staring with disbelief at his gum-covered fingers until he was led gently away, sobbing like an unrequited lover. My pal Colin was despatched to wait outside the headmaster's office where punishment was later administered; six of the best on the backside!

It is sad to relate that music lessons were abhorred by most of the school's pupils, simply because Mr. Trottman was such a nasty man. However, although my love of music was severely dented by the awful behaviour of Mr. Trottman, it somehow survived and blossomed like a resurgent flower welcoming the onset of yet another Spring.

It was at Roan School that I first became aware that I could run and run and run. The annual junior and senior cross country races took place around early June and I was selected for the junior's together with three others to represent Drake House; the worst House in the entire school at almost every activity. We set off in a pack on the three mile course which circled the outside wall of Greenwich Park until entering the park's leafy, hilly interior after about two miles. Soon, I was out ahead of the pack and finding the run really easy and, I hesitate to say, enjoyable. Boys stood around at specified places in the park as markers; their task was to direct the hundred or so runners the correct way through the undulating course. I finished first -- in a new, school record, time. My house master and fellow housemates were ecstatic. Drake House had never won anything and here we were with a first place in the annual junior cross country race. Then disaster intervened; one of the markers had sent the field in the wrong direction and the record I had set would not be allowed to stand. Instead I was told to run the junior course again on the following day when the senior's race took place. I set out on my own but had the assistance of three pacemakers sited at intervals ahead to help me complete the course, which I did and what's more, to my immense relief, I broke the school record once again!

My dad was really pleased to have a budding athlete in the family and thereafter accompanied me on many occasions when I represented the school at cross country meets throughout the surrounding area and as far south as the borders of Kent. Unfortunately my academic achievements did not match those at my primary school; except for English, French and Art, my three favourite lessons. Our English teacher a Mr. Lupiniere, known throughout the school as "Smoke-Rings" (loop-in-the-air!), was such an excellent teacher, kind and understanding as was the Art master whose name I have forgotten. French teaching was the province of "Scruffy" Milne who used to arrive at school each morning balanced precariously on a bicycle which was held together with rust. He dressed in the most outrageous of clothing, hence the nickname, Scruffy. Now, on reflection, there has to be a lesson or two to be learned here.

We have three understanding, helpful teachers achieving excellent results while a really nasty teacher, Trottman, gets awful results. Hmmm.....must have a word with the current minister for education about this.

Mum wasn't well and I was often seconded to stay home from school and look after her. My school work suffered as a result and finally, after stuttering through four and a half years of stop and start schooling, I left at aged fifteen plus a few months having sat no end-of-school examinations. I was without qualifications and about to embark on a tenuous journey into the world of work.

CHAPTER FOUR
1950-1953
FILLING IN BEFORE NATIONAL SERVICE

It was a very difficult time for school leavers in the early Fifties. The unavoidable prospect of two years compulsory National Service loomed like an indomitable brick wall placed uncompromisingly before the face of every young man contemplating a future. Already my sister and older brothers Stanley and Alfred had completed their service with, I must add, great pride. Stanley (as I have already written) was enlisted into the Royal Horse Guards and spent 18 months as part of the BAOR (British Army of the Rhine) forces in Germany. The Royal Horse Guards was a perfect regiment for Stanley since he was always meticulously smart in appearance and manner. On the other hand Alfred served his compulsory two years with the Royal Electrical and Mechanical Engineers (REME) mainly at the then British possession, the Suez Canal Zone in Egypt – once again a perfect match since he was very much into engineering with a special passion for things electrical. He was now a qualified electrician after utilising the skills he had freely acquired during his period of national service. Skills that enabled him to apply for, begin and complete an apprenticeship, at a company close to Charlton Central School where he had completed his secondary education.

He was one of many who benefited from those two compulsory years of military training because he not only learned the basics of a much in demand trade as a result of the ravages of war but he also spoke a little, gutter, Arabic that he picked up at his army base on the Sweet Water Canal, close to the Suez Canal Zone where Britain's Imperial ambitions remained solidly in place. He always smiled when reference was made to "Sweet Water" because, according to Fred's reports, the canal was nothing more than an effluent-carrying, malodorous, stream where the Arabic population risked their lives each and every time they drank its stagnant water. Raymond eventually opted for the Royal Air Force and signed up as a regular airman for a period of three years. This meant more pay and a choice of trade or profession. I'm not sure what he actually did in the Air Force but what I do know is he served his time at RAF Hendon, only a ninety minute journey from our home in Charlton. I still had a little less than three years to go before needing to face the inevitable, and three years at the tender age of fifteen seemed to stretch ahead like a lifetime. But the first thing on my mind was to find a job which, with my limited qualifications, presented quite a challenge.

I used to write long, full-of-detail, letters to my brothers and, to this day, I can still remember their military-assigned numbers. Stanley - 19153909, Alfred – 22193336, Raymond - 4068485. My number, at this stage in my life, still hadn't come up!

My resourceful mother found my first job through a contact at the Coop – the Co-operative Wholesale Society. She saved Coop stamps in a book and every year the Coop would pay a dividend. They used to hand out the stamps every time you shopped at the Coop in those days and, depending on annual profits, they would pay a dividend or the "divi" as it was known in Coop stamp-collecting circles. My mother used to send me to collect the "divi" from the Coop offices which meant standing in a long queue with lots of other scruffy kids whose mothers were either too busy or too lazy to collect it themselves. The "divi" was an annual lifeline to buy a few extras that couldn't be afforded from the regular housekeeping money.

For a reason I cannot recall, a contact at the Coop arranged for me to be interviewed for a humble clerk's position in the factory office at UGB, United Glass Bottle, manufacturers of, you've guessed it, glass bottles. There were two old men at the interview; well they looked old to a fresh-faced fifteen year old. The senior of the two was named Oldfield, who was a bit, not a lot, on the grumpy side and in his late forties. His colleague was a very quiet, gentle, slightly younger man named Briggs.

I got the job at UGB. Whether it was because of my potential glass-blowing ability or because of the intervention of the mysterious person at the Coop I shall never know. The bottle factory was about two miles from our home at Floyd Road. I walked those two miles there and two miles back every work day but it was worth it because the job proved to be interesting, satisfying and, most welcome, it put some money in my pocket even after paying for my "keep" at home. My responsibilities entailed keeping records of all the bottles made in the huge factory located on the south bank of the River Thames. I had to take orders to and bring results back from the factory floor employees. Great furnaces blasted out unbearable, searing heat that melted the materials that eventually turned into molten glass that was then transformed into bottles of all shapes and sizes on whirling machines giddily spinning around and around like mad, whirling, dervishes. The deafening noise and the extreme heat were debilitating. Can you imagine these mechanical monsters, whizzing round, shuddering wildly and clattering continually, allied to the noise of freshly blown bottles being carried off, rattling furiously, to cool before despatch throughout the country? The exhausted machines frequently broke down due to the constant, 24-hours-a-day use and the unbearable, incapacitating heat. Unfortunate engineers had to clamber all over the still warm beasts attempting to find the cause of the breakdown and then carry out repairs. Watching those men served to underline the fact that I am not an engineer, have no desire to become one and I would most definitely not have clambered over those abominable machines even if my life had depended upon it.

United Glass Bottle had a sports ground situated about three miles from where I lived in Charlton. To the young men of Floyd Road the idea of having access to an actual sports ground with lush grass on the pitch rather than split and disintegrating asphalt was heaven on Earth. UGB ran two football teams, the firsts and the reserves, both called The Pantiles. This rather incongruous name was given by one of the two dedicated men who ran the club. Imagine naming a football club after a roof tile? It's as daft as naming a football club after a day in the week and who would be daft enough to do that, I ask you Sheffield Wednesday supporters?

Since UGB didn't have enough staff who could play an acceptable level of football to form two teams I was allowed to recruit players from among my friends in Floyd Road. Naturally, the first person I approached was my best pal, good old Alan Starbuck, who, after only one game in the reserves, was immediately transferred to the first team.

Nonetheless my other pals, Percy Wright, Peter Boon, Johnny Crew and Don Temple quickly settled into the reserve side and formed the backbone of a very promising team. We played, Saturday afternoons, in the Woolwich and District League and, over a couple of bedding-in seasons, we became the team to beat.

The ground, comprising two full length football pitches and a practice ground was at the foot of Shooters Hill, in a very posh part of the area where Charlton met Woolwich, its immediate neighbouring borough; well anywhere with half decent houses that were not cracked and falling apart at the seams and with street lighting that actually worked was reckoned to be posh after the shambles that was post-war Floyd Road. The ground boasted a pavilion that housed the home and visitors changing rooms, a shower room where we could rid ourselves of the mud accumulated during the game and another area where tea and cakes were served after the match. After the bombed out area on the corner of Floyd Road where we played head tennis, the UGB ground was our Wembley Stadium. Not without cost however; we each had to pay a small amount after every game towards the match fee given to referees without whom each game would have sunk to the level of a street brawl.

We used to turn up for matches at least an hour before kick off time; we'd spend so much time loosening up before the game that by the time the opening whistle was blown, we'd all be exhausted and on our knees. Nevertheless, we still invariably won and indeed went on to complete a couple of seasons unbeaten. Those were rich, fulfilling days; sixteen years old and playing football on a real pitch covered with lush, green grass was my idea of football heaven.

My love affair with Charlton Athletic, the local professional team, inexplicably blossomed in due proportion to their season-by-season failures. Back in 1947 they won the FA Cup, beating Burnley 1-0 with a goal from a tricky Scottish left-winger name of Chris Duffy. I remember running out into Floyd Road after listening to the commentary on the BBC Home programme. I fully expected to see the road crowded with rejoicing folk, waving Charlton flags and twirling rattles. Nothing stirred beyond the local, mangy dogs sniffing in the gutters for particles of food. I was both amazed and saddened. This was before the days of television of course so perhaps not too many supporters were listening to the radio commentary since it was often a tedious, Oxford-accented commentary that was anathema and often incomprehensible to the locals with their strangled south London accents. But, nevertheless, 1-0 in any accent was good news and I therefore lost no time in informing everyone I came across that unloved, lowly Charlton, the poor relations of London's football clubs, had won the FA Cup for the first time in its history. The ubiquitous newspaper vendors arrived later the same evening carrying copies of the Star, News and Standard; three competing newspapers circulating every day throughout the length and breadth of London. There it was, confirmed in black-and-white banner headlines on the front page and repeated on sports pages at the back of each newspaper:

CHARLTON WIN THE F.A. CUP

Since that date Charlton's successes are as rare as the rarest of fillet steaks -- that is unless it can be deemed a success that they managed to retain a place in the First Division of the Football League. Whatever, my love for the team saw me standing on the mountainous terraces behind Sam Bartram's goal at every home game. The player's names still excite me whenever they spring to mind. Don Welsh, Harold Hobbis, Jock Campbell, Jack Shreeve, Bert Johnson, Sailor Brown, Benny Fenton, Charlie Vaughan, Gordon Hurst, Derek Ufton, Eddie Firmani. In those days professional footballers were paid twenty pounds a week, plus a bonus of two pounds for a win and a one pound bonus for a draw. The price of admission to the game, paid at the turnstiles, was one shilling and sixpence!

I made some welcome pocket money on match days by looking after some of the spectator's push bikes. There was a walled-in area in front of 17 Floyd Road and the adjoining pavement that was ideal for safe storage of a number of bikes, especially so since I had trained (don't laugh) Gyp to sit on guard during the two hours or so of the spectator's arriving, the 90 minutes of play and the spectator's departure. I used to attach her lead (we now had a posh leather lead attached to a strap around her neck where her name and address was engraved on a metal plate) to the handle bars of the last of the fifteen or so bikes being looked after. One match day, after being disturbed by the snarling of a neighbour's dog, Gyp took off after the dog like a pack of Huskies dragging a sledge. The bicycle was dragged down Floyd Road and ended up with its wheels lodged either side of a lamp post with Gyp still straining against her lead in a futile attempt to silence the offending dog. All the money I earned on that particular day went on paying for repairs to the bicycle plus the cost of treatment for Gyp's strained neck at the local veterinary!

Gyp was a dog with a mind of her own. This may have been due to the effects of the near death experience she suffered before Alfred and I rescued her from a watery grave. Whatever, she didn't like being taken for walks, preferring her own company. So whenever she felt the need she would let us know by a peculiar sound she had developed. It wasn't a bark, it wasn't a whine but rather something in between, a kind of barky whine! As soon as we heard the I-want-to-go-out sound escape her open jaws one of us would open the front door and let her out into the street where she would disappear in a blur of doggedness, presumably heading for the nearest lamp post. Some hours later we would hear a loud, continuous, scratching at the front door – Gyp was back from her daily wanderings! The already dilapidated front door became a multi-rutted mess down one side where her razor sharp claws had scraped so frequently and assiduously over the weeks and months.

In the same row of shops where the Starbuck family ran a greengrocer shop was a general store owned by a young woman called Maud. The shop stocked butter, eggs, sugar, bread, sweets, etcetera in lick smacking abundance. The problem was our ration books only allowed the purchase of the government allotted amount each week. The cherished ration book contained a sequence of pages with A, B. C. D and E stamps; each stamp was assigned a value, which was frequently changed by the government in terms of what and how much of a commodity each stamp could buy. To give an idea of how much the rationing allowed each person, here is a typical example of what we were allowed in an often failed attempt to fill the space in our empty bellies.

Bacon and ham -- two ounces (57 gm) per person every two weeks. Cheese -- one and a half ounces (43 gm) a week. Butter/margarine -- seven ounces (198 gm) a week. Cooking fats -- two ounces (57 gm) a week. Meat -- one shilling's (five new pence) worth a week. Sugar -- eight ounces (227 gm) a week. Tea -- two ounces (57 gm) a week. Chocolates and sweets -- four ounces (113 gm) a week. With eggs there was no fixed ration, although one egg for each ration book was the practice whenever they became available. Liquid milk was limited to three pints a week, while jam and preserves topped out at four ounces (113 gm) a week. Bread, soap, bananas, and oranges were also rationed during this period. In 1951 the UK populace could only buy 10 pence (four new pence) worth of meat each week. Then, to everyone's astonishment, just when it appeared as if rationing was about to end, two new commodities became subject to rationing a year after the war ended. Bread was rationed from 1946 to 1948 and even the poor old common potato was rationed for a year from

1947. The much despised points system ended in 1950 although rationing continued for a further four years until 1954 when meat was finally de-rationed!

How my mother managed to produce any semblance of a square meal each day I really cannot say. And yet she somehow managed to produce on occasion my favourite meal, minced beef, which she somehow contrived to make as tasty as anything produced by Delia Smith. Swimming in a bath of delicious gravy, the minced beef was further enhanced to mouth-watering tastes of pure delight by a large onion floating grandiosely, like an errant iceberg, in a sea of bubbling brown liquid. If anyone is having problems thinking of a suitable epitaph for my gravestone it could be: "He loved his mother's minced beef."

An embryonic thought in closing. I assume the word "obese" wasn't introduced into the English language until decades later when people began stuffing themselves to excess on pre-cooked sugar and salt impregnated meals three times a day while munching in between times on packets of crisps and chocolate biscuits while drinking cans of beer and coke, when reclining half the day and night sprawled on sofas watching the inane antics of nobodies competing for attention in the Big Brother house, the mind-blowing wannabee celebs cavorting on X Factor and the never-ending succession of soaps epitomised by Eastenders and Coronation Street! Yet another emerging thought! The re-introduction of rationing would see the weight and size of the population of Britain reduced within months to that of wartime, slim, svelte, human beings who could actually move around more quickly, and with more finesse, than a trodden upon slug!

In spite of everything that should have dictated against it, my health and that of my brothers was pretty good except for the odd bout of influenza, sore throat, common cold -- all that mundane, non-serious, stuff. That is until I began to notice a swelling in the left hand side of my neck, just below the chin. The swelling grew bigger by the week and mum eventually decided it prudent to pay a visit to Dr. Bailey, our local GP whose surgery was but a ten minute stroll from Floyd Road. His diagnosis was a trifle scary! Tubercular Cervical Adentis; apparently the gland in my neck was infected by mycobacteria which causes tuberculosis; the most dreaded disease abroad at the time and apparently there was no prevailing, effective, antibiotic according to our GP. And what was even scarier was the proposed remedy -- an operation to drain the relevant gland at St. Bartholomew's Hospital at West Smithfield in the City of London.

St. Barts, as it is fondly known, was ready to admit me almost immediately so, casting aside all fears, doubts, I was escorted on a succession of trams and buses to the hospital by my worried mum who stayed with me until I was comfortably settled in a lovely clean bed in one of the hospital's many wards.

All I can remember of the operation was lying recumbent on an operating table, with the anaesthetist asking me to start counting up to ten. By the time I reached three I was gone, under the influence of a drug that brought blessed relief from the anxiety I had been harbouring. When I came to I was back in my bed in the ward. I had a bandage swathed around my neck through which a small rubber tube was protruding. Honey coloured liquid was oozing from the tube, staining the white bandage.

'How are you feeling?' asked a man bending over me whom I assumed to be a doctor.

I nodded my head, trusting the action taken by my head indicated I was feeling quite well.

'We've put some stitches in your neck,' continued the doctor. 'And we'll have to keep the drain in your neck for a few days until there is no more seepage. Then we will arrange for you to go home where a nurse will call upon you every day to administer injections which will help you fully recover.'

I was unable to speak, probably due to a combination of nerves, sore throat and the tight bandage restricting any movement of my neck. So once again I merely nodded my understanding of the situation and hoped the grateful look in my eyes adequately conveyed my thanks.

With a gentle pat on my seventeen-year-old head the doctor left my bedside and continued his task of assuring the ward's other patients that they were in good, safe, reliable hands. I knew I was going to be fine, because mum arrived the same evening smiling brightly, her presence lighting my bed space. She brought a present for me (a small bar of milk chocolate) which she tucked with care into the bedside drawer awaiting the moment when I could begin to eat things solid once more.

To this day I have a long scar streaking my neck that reminds me, as I shave each day, how close I came to joining the thousands of unfortunates who died as a result of a disease from which I had been fortuitously reprieved.

After I arrived home post-operation the realisation of the awful conditions in which we were living was further reinforced by the recollection of the antiseptic purity and scrubbed cleanliness of the hospital ward I had left behind. As promised, a very efficient nurse dressed in an immaculate blue and white uniform called each day and, after a few moments of efficacious preparation, stuck a very painful needle into my resisting bottom. Gyp, highly interested in this new arrival on her previously inviolable scene, would sniff noisily around her feet whenever she arrived, she would try to lick the nurses' face as she bent over me and generally managed to make a hairy nuisance of herself.

CHAPTER FIVE
1953-1956
EXTENDED NATIONAL SERVICE

My brother Ray completed his three years in the Royal Air Force in 1954, eleven months after I decided to follow in his footsteps by signing on for three years as a regular. Consequently, for a period, we were both serving our country at the same time; two Garlands facing the UK's enemies should be sufficient cause for hundreds of thousands of white flags to be raised aloft in submissive surrender! Right, enough of the fantasy, now for the reality!

RAF Cardington in Bedfordshire was the first stop after the initial signing on process which took place at government buildings in Marston, a suburb of Oxford. After medical checks (some very embarrassing) at Marston we were transferred to Cardington where I and my fellow recruits were kitted out with a uniform, assorted items of clothing and equipment. I was delighted, I was now in possession of more clothing than I had ever owned in my short life. Being given (new) stuff wasn't something I was used to and I felt a sense of acute embarrassment as the pile I was carrying on my forearms grew so high I had to peer around the side of the pile in order to make my way to the next delivery point. I was beginning to warm to the idea of the coming three years during which I would be cosseted by really friendly men wearing blue uniforms who insisted on handing me lots of exciting goodies for absolutely nothing. Was my life about to take a turn for the better?

RAF West Kirby was our designated basic training camp. Alongside 17 other "sprogs" (a slang term for new recruits) plus a kindly Sergeant named Gary, we boarded a train at Cardington and headed northwest towards Liverpool main line station where we were met by the man who was to be our DI (drill instructor) for the next 12 weeks. It was an awakening of the rudest kind! Corporal Crowe was the epitome of in-your-face, don't-say-a-word-or-I'll-cut-your-tongue-out, screaming, cursing, maniacal, drill instructor. CC, as he became known, hustled us aboard an RAF lorry where we sat perched uncomfortably on benches that ran along either side of the lorry, bouncing up and down, scared to utter a word, trembling, praying for deliverance from what was about to come. My brother Ray was uppermost in my mind; he never once mentioned the Hell that goes by the name of basic training – but I, we, all eighteen of us, were about to experience how hard were the facts of life for raw recruits in Her Majesty's armed forces!

Row upon row of elongated huts, seemingly never ending, stretched into the late-April murk that greeted us as we passed the guard room at the imposing entrance to RAF West Kirby. My already sunken heart was now at the level of the Titanic as she came to rest at the bottom of the Atlantic. Despondent, depressed, pessimistic, miserable -- where was my mummy when I needed her most?

CC marched us, kitbags on shoulders, into billet number 204, our home from home for the next three months. Lined up either side of the hut were eighteen beds on which were placed sad mattresses looking like grey slabs of concrete. Beside each bed was a small wooden cupboard, next to which stood a narrow wardrobe in matching wood. In the middle of the hut was a large table with long benches on either side. At each end was a cast iron stove, gleaming bright as a burnished dark grey button, the result of the efforts of a generation of former recruits plus the daily application of gallons of black lead polish. A voluminous coal scuttle, also glinting brightly, was placed to the rear of each stove. The stove's chimney, stretching like a petrified serpent seeking an exit through the roof of the billet, was burnished to the same colour of grey/black quartz.

We were assigned our bed spaces. My space, the first one on the right from the separate outside room where CC was privately accommodated, was strategically placed because it was from this position that the appointed senior man, yours truly, was supposed to maintain control over seventeen other raw recruits. Yes, CC had identified my less than obvious leadership qualities and dumped me with the onerous task of keeping order when he was absent. It was akin to appointing our dog Gyp to look after Charlton Athletic supporters bicycles! After being issued with bedding, then having an evening meal at the cookhouse, finding the camp's NAAFI, we were free until reveille tomorrow morning. I had a terrible first night. I am loathe to admit it but……I wet the bed. Yes, I woke from a nightmare to find myself in a very damp, smelly bed. What could I do? Think, think – how do I escape unscathed from this potentially life-changing, highly embarrassing situation? I carefully bundled up the sheets and made for the nearby shower room where I had, upon arrival, noticed radiators emitting heat. I was not sure what the time was but I recall it was pitch black outside the billet, not a single light was visible to help me on my way. I stumbled along to the shower room and, thank the Lord, the heating was on! I placed the sheets over two of the radiators and settled down beside one of them shivering, not from the cold but from a hitherto undetected defect in my tried and tested bladder. I was a hopeless, sobbing, useless wreck. Suffice to say I managed to dry the sheets and returned them to my bed without waking anybody. If CC had been roused he would have had me drawn and quartered in front of the entire regiment! Senior man? More diuretic boy!

Square-bashing. "British informal military drill performed repeatedly on a barrack square." The Concise Oxford English Dictionary's description, while technically correct, does not reflect reality. It doesn't mention screaming drill instructors; it doesn't mention the damage done to the feet or to the boots belonging to me and my fellow recruits; it doesn't mention hours spent "bulling" boots to a shine equalling that of the most assiduous member of the Royal Horse Guards. A task that became wasted as rain, grit and mud trashed our efforts during those square bashing sessions.

Up at six each morning, followed by a rush to get to the showers before the hot water runs out and transforms the shower into an ice-cold watery Hell. A mad scramble back to the billet before clambering into uniforms as stiff and scratchy as the roughest of sandpapers, closely followed by the arranging of one's bed and bed-space into the approved orderly condition. Then a wild rush to the cookhouse for a breakfast of eggs, bacon, and sausages washed down with a mug of tea, swiftly followed by a prompt return to the billet to prepare for the most taxing of duties – the daily kit inspection; two hours of unrelenting pressure, five days of each and every week.

Group Captain Worthington walked into our billet looking as if he was embarking on a mission to eradicate all of the eighteen sprogs standing to attention at the end of their respective beds. He carried a highly polished stick in his right hand which he pushed every now and again into his left hand's palm as if trying to puncture it. He was accompanied by CC who was standing ram-rod straight, unmoving. He looked as if someone had rammed a series of scaffold poles into his immaculately pressed uniform. First in line for the duo's attention was (senior man, diuretic boy) yours truly. I tried to control my nervousness which was causing an occasional twitch to appear on my right cheek. The Group Captain looked me up and down, several times. He then moved to see whether I had arranged the stack of bed clothes on my mattress in the approved fashion. He took his polished stick, thrust it into the stack and dragged it apart. He turned to CC. 'Make sure this doesn't happen again corporal. It is your responsibility to ensure everything is laid out according to regulations. Now let's move on.'

The Group Captain and CC continued inspecting the other seventeen beds. Each one suffered the same fate as did mine. Now the billet looked like a second hand clothes shop after a horde of bargain hunters had visited, found nothing worth purchasing and departed empty-handed. Group Captain Worthington stood aghast, shaking his head. His peaked cap almost fell off. He grabbed it, settled it firmly back on his head, turned around, whispered harshly into CC's ear and departed the billet leaving our dear, red-faced, Corporal looking like a stick of dynamite about to explode. I knew we were in for a rough ride. He turned, thrust his face close to mine and yelled so loud that my mum back in London could have heard it.

'You call yourself a bloody Senior Man? What a bloody shambles that turned out to be. You were supposed to have made sure everyone had their kit laid out according to bleeding regulations!'

He looked around the billet. My fellow occupants, all seventeen standing rigidly to attention, were obviously just as shocked as was I.

'Right,' he said, his shaking voice now almost back to normal. 'Everybody listen and listen well! I will conduct another kit inspection in one hour's time. If everything isn't A1 I will put you all on report. Which means you'll all be confined to barracks for the coming weekend. You'll be the last to attend meals, if there's any food left that is, and there'll be extra square bashing. So, get on with it -- kit inspection in one hour's time.'

The thought of extra square bashing (marching up and down the station's huge parade ground, having CC shout and scream at us, and all because we sprogs still cannot march in step, or turn around in unison) acted as an overwhelming impetus to get our kit in the correct order. One frantic hour passed before CC returned. He marched into the billet and inspected the eighteen beds, nodding occasionally as he saw the improvement in everyone's kit lay out. He finally arrived at my bed, bent forward, and looked me squarely in the eye.

'Well done,' he said displaying a grudging grin. 'Let's not have this happen again in front of the Group Captain or I'll have your guts for garters.'

Slowly, very slowly, we eighteen sprogs were transformed into something approaching a military unit. It took ten long weeks of unremitting slog before the occupants of billet 204 gained sufficient self-confidence to consider themselves capable of taking part in our passing-out parade scheduled for two weeks' time. The bi-weekly passing-out parade was frighteningly familiar to those sprogs who arrived at West Kirby at the same time as me. Every two weeks we were assembled around the parade ground to witness the passing-out of those hundred or so trainees whose tenure at West Kirby preceded ours by some weeks. Come rain, wind, snow, sunshine, the parade was unavoidable. It demonstrated the culmination of all the training we had received. Sprogs transformed into something akin to the finished article who reacted to the orders of their superiors immediately and without question. It was, in addition, an unambiguous demonstration of how innocent young lads can be turned into confident men.

The parade went without mishap. I recall (as Senior Man) marching solo towards our Commanding Officer to receive a passing-out banner; a pole upon which the regimental flag was fluttering proudly. I marched back to the spot on the parade ground where my seventeen colleagues were standing rigidly to attention, lined up facing the centre of the parade ground. I joined them and stood to attention until the regimental band began playing the theme from The Dam Buster's, the Royal Air Force's most popular marching music. The regimental Sergeant Major gave the order to right turn and then to quick march. Ten separate groups of eighteen airmen marched off in unison following the band. It was a proud moment in time and something which would live long in our memories.

The passing out parade occurred a week prior to the coronation of Queen Elizabeth II. It was decided that our contingent would be used to line the route when the newly crowned Queen was scheduled to visit Wales. So, off we were shipped to Llangollen where the Royal visit and route-lining was to take place. I was distraught because I was missing my family and friends and wanted them to see me in my uniform but it was not to be, at least until the Welsh visit was over. Came the day of the visit and we were each designated a spot on the route where would stand, rifle with bayonet in place, ready for the order to perform the Royal present-arms salute, as the Queen and her entourage passed. Embarrassingly a mischievous, teen-age, female spectator stuck an orange on the end of my bayonet just as the Royal carriage was about to pass my section of the route. I was unable to remove the orange because we were in the stand-at-ease position, and to move a muscle at this critical point in time would have seen me placed under arrest and become the unwilling guest of the feared, white-capped, RAF Military Police. The entourage neared and we were first given the order to stand to attention and then another order to adopt the Royal salute, present-arms, position. Spectators were pointing and laughing while others were snapping me with their cameras as the orange atop my bayonet was raised in salute. A photo of me appeared in the local paper the next day alongside those of the Queen and her entourage. I trust she saw my photograph and found it in her heart to have a Royal chuckle at my expense.

After a week spent at home with family and friends I took the train to Cardiff, where I was due to begin the next part of my training at nearby RAF St. Athan. I was only 13 weeks into the three years I had signed up for, and I was already beginning to doubt whether I had been right to sign on for the extra year. Okay, I know I was being paid more than those who were on national service but, believe me, the difference was minimal. St. Athan was a short lived posting. I was immediately at odds with the Welshman I was supposed to replacing when his national service ended in a month's time. His name escapes me but what I do remember to this day were his constant attempts to make me look stupid in front of the Flight Lieutenant to whom we were assigned. He took to calling me "Punchy" presumably because he was aware that I had been a keen amateur boxer before joining the RAF. In his warped mind he was associating the punches one received during a boxing match to his labeling me as being stupid. I finally settled the issue between us by inviting him to meet me in the boxing ring located in the station's gymnasium. A horde of his supporters turned up for the fight expecting him to prevail. It was over in two rounds. I was all over him and he quit, blood streaming from a broken nose!

A few days later I was told I was to be transferred to RAF Hereford, the station that was home to the Strategic Air Service, or SAS as it is known throughout the world. Not that I was about to join that illustrious band of men, instead I was on course for something somewhat less demanding. I was about to become a trainee for the RAF Regiment, a division of the RAF whose prime duty is to guard its bases spread around the globe. Perhaps my boxing prowess was to be utilised to the RAF's advantage? I asked myself the question and answered no. The reason I was being transferred was purely and simply because I had given a bloody nose to somebody who deserved it, unequivocally. As a consequence, I determined to make the most of what was in store for me and do my best to become a credit to the RAF.

RAF Hereford was totally different to St Athan. An abounding sense of fortitude was abroad throughout the camp. Although I did not come face to face with the SAS who were billeted in a secluded section known as Bradbury

Lines, I met my RAF Regiment colleagues and commenced training under a sergeant named Jamie Roberts. He was tough but fair and I took to him as does a bee to a pot of honey. Weapon training was his forte and it wasn't long before I became a grade one marksman. Alongside weapon training there were a variety of other challenges including never-ending trekking through snow-clad Welsh mountains and settling down for a freezing night in a bivouac alongside my new comrades. I came through the three month course with flying colours and received my first promotion – I was now a lance corporal (acting)!

The rest of my tenure in the Royal Air Force is best set aside. After serving at a number of different camps in the UK, the day of my release could not come soon enough. It seems to me that, while National Service was a necessary evil at the time, it was ill conceived. Young boys, fresh out of basic training, lost their lives in far off places such as Korea while fighting to free that country of a yoke imposed by communists who were intent upon imposing their autocratic style of government throughout South East Asia. Many of my friends were involved in the fighting there, including a life-long pal, Peter Collins, who served with distinction in the Parachute Regiment, one of Britain's most revered regiments. Fortunately he survived unscathed, but hundreds did not. Today Korea is divided by the 38th parallel. The bottom half, South Korea, remains a democracy supported by those western nations who fought for its future, and the upper half, North Korea, is ruled with an iron fist by one of the most hideous of autocratic regimes the world has ever known.

CHAPTER SIX

1956 to 1984

FLEET STREET

A couple of weeks after completing my service in the RAF I set out to seek employment. After the cushy life I had become used to during the past three years, I now had to earn a living, not only for myself but also for my parents who were finding it hard to exist on dad's weekly wage. Sister Vera was still serving as a regular in the WRNS (Women's Royal Navy Service), brothers Stan, Fred and Ray were gainfully employed and contributing to the family income. Now I had to do the same.

I cannot recall why, but I found myself wandering past an employment agency in London's Fleet Street. I looked in the window to see what was available for someone with my limited educational background. My eyes lighted upon an advertisement that interested me. It was placed by a company called United Press International. They were seeking a junior to help out in the newsroom. I was twenty-one, still a junior I suppose, and the world of news was one in which I had a professed interest. So I stepped into the agency's tiny office and enquired after the position. The young girl seated behind the sole desk smiled welcomingly as I approached her.

'Can I help you?' she asked.

I nodded and sat down before replying. 'You have an ad in the window for a junior with United Press International. I'm very interested. Do you think I could get an interview while I'm here in London?'

The young lady smiled again before opening one of the desk's drawers. She withdrew a thick folder which she placed on the desk accompanied by yet another smile. 'Let's take a look,' she said. She shuffled through the mass of paper in the folder and stopped at one which she picked up and placed on top of the folder. 'Here it is,' she said. She read the contents to herself before looking up at me. 'Can you tell be about your background please? You know, education, work experience, that kind of thing?'

I told her my name and that I had attended the Roan Grammar School in Greenwich from aged eleven until I was sixteen, obtaining passes in GCE (General Certificate of Education) with A's in English, Mathematics and History plus B's in Art and German. (Attending Roan Grammar School was true of course but, please forgive me Jesus, I lied with fingers crossed about having passed several GCE's). She appeared to be impressed, if the constant nodding of her head was any indication. I then told her about my three years in the RAF which, once again, received several nods of approval. 'I think you fit the profile of the person UPI is looking for. Let me see if I can make an appointment for you.' She picked up the phone and dialed a number. It was answered quickly. 'I have a young man here, Dennis Garland, who I think would be ideally suited for the position of junior. Is there any chance he could come to see you now?' The voice at the other end of the line was indistinct. However, from the look on the young lady's face, I assumed the answer was "yes."

'Good news,' she said with a smile that lit the office. 'You can go now, to 8 Bouverie Street, 2nd floor, ask at reception for Dick Growald. He's the European and Middle East Editor, an American.' She stood up shook my hand. 'Off you go now and good luck. Let me know how you get on.'

Bouverie Street is off Fleet Street and, alongside other assorted companies, housed the headquarters not only of UPI but also the News of the World and the Evening Standard. If, when, I get the job I will be working in close proximity to some of the biggest names in the exciting world of newspaper publishing. This provided added impetus to my eager feet as they carried me the hundred yards or so down Fleet Street, before turning right into Bouverie Street where I found the UPI office situated on the right-hand side. I was feeling nervous and unsure as I climbed two flights of stairs to the second floor. I entered through an oak double door, turned left, and my eyes widened as I saw the huge room stretching into the far distance. The clatter of typewriters and teleprinters was accompanied by loud voices straining to be heard above the noise. The reception desk was unstaffed. My nervousness was now climbing to new heights. Fortunately a young woman appeared and approached me. 'Can I help you?' she asked in a friendly way. 'Er yes, I'm here to see Mr. Growald, about a job.' She nodded. 'His office is over there on the right hand side. Go and see if he's there. If not came back and I'll find him for you.'

A man I assumed to be Dick Growald was seated in a window-fringed office browsing through a stack of newspapers. He looked up when I tentatively tapped on the door and motioned for me to enter by means of a flickering, hooked finger.

The interview was shorter and sweeter than I had anticipated. Dick Growald was an archetypal American: confident, to the point, quick to reach a decision. He asked me a series of questions which I answered as truthfully as I was able. He asked about my service in the RAF and appeared satisfied with my rather hasty summing up. 'Right,' he said. 'You're hired. Report to me next Monday nine o'clock and we'll go see management up on the fourth floor and get you signed up for the best international news agency in the world.' He stood up and looked at a scrap of paper on which were scribbled some words. 'Oh, one other

thing, I see your first name is Dennis. That's a problem ---
we have three persons named Dennis in the newsroom
already.' He saw me raise my eyebrows. 'No arguments,'
he said, dismissing my unstated objection. 'As of now you
will be known at UPI as David.'

I was about to be employed. A new job plus a new
name were confronting me. Was I up to it? "Of course I
am," I muttered to myself over and over as I made my way
home. "It's only a question of applying myself to
something which fate has thrown my way."

CHAPTER SEVEN

I had no idea what a junior was supposed to do in and around a hyper-active news room but I soon found out.

My duties included running errands, fetching and carrying at everyone's behest, answering telephones, ripping news items from stuttering teleprinters and delivering them to the news desk, constantly running up two flights of stairs to the photo department with requests to forward photographs to accompany a current news item and, very occasionally, sitting down at a typewriter (computers were not yet installed in newsrooms) while attempting to compose informative, interesting news stories.

Fortunately, regarding the latter, I had a very patient, experienced mentor named Harry Hobbs who helped me re-write news stories submitted by UPI's stringers, most of whom were semi-illiterate when it came to writing in English, rather than in their own language. Once stories were complete they were passed to a teleprinter operator who would transcribe them and send them on their way to subscribing newspapers throughout the world.

The first year passed swiftly in an exhausting blur of working up to twelve hours a day, sometimes six days a week. But I didn't mind. I was employed doing something I really loved and that was all that mattered. An order to attend a meeting in Dick Growald's office provided an unexpected lift in my ambition to become a full time journalist.

'Good morning David,' he said. 'Take a seat.' On his desk were cuttings which I thought I recognised as some of the many stories I had written over the past few months. He picked up the top one and read it to himself.

'Right,' he said, putting the cutting down. 'You have done extremely well over the past year and I think the time has arrived for you to work full time on the news desk. You'll have to help your replacement settle in and, once that's done, you'll make the switch. It'll be eight hours shift work of course, but I am sure you'll settle in quickly.' He stood up and held out a hand which I grasped and shook with genuine warmth.

'Good luck,' he said. 'And don't let me down.'

The following four years were never less than exciting. Although stationed permanently in London I worked for spells of varying length at the UPI offices in New York, Rome, Brussels, Frankfurt, Lisbon, Tel Aviv, Warsaw, Nicosia, Stockholm and Oslo, to name a few. Then, quite unexpectedly, I was asked by the then current European and Middle East Vice President, Julius Humi, whether I would consider switching to the business side of UPI. In other words I would be involved in selling UPI's services (i.e. news, news pictures, television news and features) to existing and potential clients throughout Europe and the Middle East. It was a difficult decision but I decided it was time to try something different. I was very close to Julius Humi from the time when he was managing UPI's news picture service out of London. He and his family lived at Shortlands which is adjacent to Bromley, Kent. Coincidentally my wife Patricia and I once had a flat in the same district and we often met Julius and his lovely Italian wife Gabriella when out shopping in the teeming metropolis which is Bromley. Their son Peter was at college while their daughter, very sad to say, suffered from mental problems. Why is it that really nice people have more than their fair share of problems, while those who don't give a damn get away, apparently, scot free? Life is certainly strange and such questions will never be answered because as everyone knows, you have to accept whatever arrives on your doorstep and deal with it.

I told Julius I would be proud to represent UPI in its business dealings with existing and new clients, and thereby began a new phase in my working life. The combination of my first-hand knowledge of UPI's news products and my ability to explain how and why these products would benefit clients led to an increase in UPI's client base over the next three years. Alongside UPI's own news products I also became involved with a UPI subsidiary known as United Features Syndicate. Everything from world class comic strips, including Peanuts and Garfield, to topical, feature-length, articles was included in its brief. In the latter respect I reported to a charming Swedish woman named Elsie Aspman who, although on UPI's payroll, managed the burgeoning interests of United

Feature Syndicate. The switch from newsroom (and the alternating shifts) to business meant a change of work space. Instead of the bustling newsroom, I was now situated in a quiet office on the 3rd floor. I felt quite lonely and often found myself descending the flight of stairs leading to the second floor from where I could see my former friends and colleagues hard at work. Had I made the right decision? Waves of doubt flooded my brain and were only assuaged by poring over existing clients' contracts and taking careful notes as to when, how and if the contracts were to be renewed. I was also free of the demands of the shift system, could reasonably expect to be home at a reasonable hour, thereby giving me time to pursue an activity dear to my heart; finding a soul mate before old age intervened.

CHAPTER EIGHT

We met when I was twenty-four and she a mere eighteen years of age. The Lyceum in London's Strand was a venue where the then current vogue for ballroom dancing was assiduously satisfied on Friday and Saturday evenings. I was with my pal Peter Jeffries and two girls whom we had met at the same ballroom a week previously. It was our first date together and we were determined to impress them with our worldly knowledge of the London dance scene. That was until I saw her at the other end of the long counter where people were checking in their coats for safekeeping until this evening's dancing reached its close. Our eyes met and an unspoken message was transmitted in an instant. She was so pretty. Her auburn hair was flicked up around her neck and over her ears. She was wearing a close-fitting, dark green tweed, two piece suit, the bottom half of which covered her knees. On her feet were copper coloured high-heeled shoes. The overall effect was, in my open-mouthed opinion, very close to my idea of womanly perfection!

Check-in complete, she turned around and motioned to a girl standing at her rear. After a quick smile directed at me, she and her companion disappeared through the gilt-framed double door which led to the already swirling dance floor. I turned to face Peter.

'Did you see that Pete? She smiled at me!'

'I had to smile he first time I saw you,' he answered, grinning at his quick riposte. Pete, anxious to consolidate a week-old liaison with his chosen partner for the evening, continued. 'Come on, the girls are ready; let's go to the balcony upstairs for a drink.' It was from our seats around a table on the balcony that I could see her seated beside a young woman on a settee situated just off the dance floor. They were talking animatedly, pointing, laughing, smiling, and obviously intent upon having an enjoyable evening. A man of about my age walked up to her and, I assume, asked her for a dance. She declined with a smile and a shake of the head. I was now very concerned that she would be asked to dance, she'd accept and my chance to meet and introduce myself to her would be history. Determined to turn a fortuitous meeting into something more consequential, I turned to Pete and whispered in his ear. 'I'm going down to ask her to dance. Don't tell the girls. I won't be long.'

I muttered an excuse to the girls. Can't remember exactly what it was; perhaps it was something about buying chocolates. I winked at Pete, left the table and headed for the stairs leading to the ballroom. She was still seated on the settee but her friend was gone; probably she'd been asked to dance. As I approached, buttoning up the jacket of my navy blue pin-striped suit, she looked up, surprise evident on her pretty face.

'Would you like to dance?' A wavering voice betrayed my attempt to sound cool and confident. She rose to her feet, nodded, and headed for the dance floor with me trailing in her wake. I looked up to the balcony and could see Pete and the girls chatting, occasionally sipping their drinks. I placed a palm over the side of my face in an attempt at disguise. Luck was on my side, they didn't see me. The band was playing a waltz; the only dance I could perform in time, using the correct steps, and without squashing a partner's toes beneath my size ten shoes. As we danced I tried to make sure I was not visible to the threesome on the balcony; this meant skulking down behind the bodies of other dancers while trying to maintain a sense of decorum with my, as yet, unnamed dancing partner. She followed my sporadic glances at the balcony, which caused tiny creases to appear on her forehead.

'Is there something bothering you,' she asked. 'Why do you keep bobbing up and down?'

I tried my best to appear nonchalant. 'My friend Pete is up there in the balcony with his girlfriend and her sister. He asked me to make up a foursome which I wasn't too pleased about but I am now because I've met you.'

The enigmatic look on my dance partner's face had been replaced by something a little closer to a smile. 'You men,' she said. 'Always ready with a smooth chat up line.' I knew I had to act quickly because I could see Pete up on his feet, staring down at the packed dance floor. 'Oh no, my pal's getting restless. I'll have to go when the dance is over.' I was determined this jewel of a girl would not get away. 'This is so frustrating,' I said. 'I don't even know your name, or anything about you.'

The closing bars of "Lady in Red" brought the dance to an end, whereupon we meandered back to the seat where her friend was waiting, a big welcoming smile on her face. 'Hello,' she said, standing up. 'And who is this?' My dancing partner shook her head. 'I don't know his name but I'm sure he'll tell us if I ask.'

I laughed before answering. 'I'm Dennis, sometimes known as Denny, also Den and, at work, I'm David. Plus other names I will refrain from mentioning. And your name is….?' I stared into my dance partner's twinkling brown eyes. 'Patricia, Patricia Norman and this (she indicated towards her friend) is my best friend Denise. We are both hair stylists at a salon called Martin Douglas in Davis Street, next to Claridge's Hotel. But that's enough about us, what about you? What is your surname?'

I smiled. 'Garland.'

'Oh really, like Judy Garland,' replied Patricia. 'Are you related?'

'Of course, she's my grandmother!'

'Are you serious?'

I was about to reply when Pete appeared through the doorway, annoyance visibly apparent on his face.

'Come on,' he said, confronting me while ignoring the girls, 'we are fed up waiting and if you don't join us now, we're leaving.' He turned around and disappeared the way he had come. I did my best to look unconcerned.

'As you can see girls, I have to go.' I addressed Patricia. 'Will it be okay if I call you at your salon after the weekend?'

Receiving a nod accompanied by a smile, I shook hands with the girls and began walking towards the stairs leading to the balcony. I stopped and looked over my shoulder. 'By the way Patricia, just so you know, I'm going to marry you!'

The following Monday I was in the office and itching to call Patricia. I was constantly being interrupted by work colleagues every time I went to call Directory Enquiries. I decided to shut my office door; which I rarely do because when wide open it allows me to see what is going on in the UPI corridors of power! I sat down behind my desk and picked up the phone. The operator quickly located the number for Martin Douglas. I took a deep breath and dialled the number. It was answered at the first ring.

'Martin Douglas hair salon, can I help you?'

'Er yes, I would like to speak to Patricia Norman please.'

'Patricia Norman? Do you mean Pat Norman? She isn't known as Patricia as far as I know.'

'Oh, what's in a name?' I answered brightly. 'Pat is short for Patricia, so it must be the same person.'

'If you'd like to hold I will see if she is available to talk to you.'

I heard much background mumbling before a feminine voice entered my left ear. 'Who is this?' asked the voice. I tried to contain my excitement.

'It's Dennis, we met at The Lyceum on Saturday.'

There was a lengthy pause before the voice said. 'I'm sorry but I've never been to The Lyceum and I certainly do not know anyone called.......what did you say your name was?'

I repeated my name. 'No, sorry, I have no idea who you are, unless....'

I latched onto the voice's last word. 'Unless? Unless what?'

'Unless you mean **Gill** Norman! She's my cousin-in-law whose real name is Patricia but she is known at Martin Douglas as Gill. Come to think of it she mentioned The Lyceum during coffee break this morning. Said she'd met someone. Can you hold on a minute while I check with her?'

The minute stretched to several and, to make things more difficult, my pursuit of Patricia was suddenly interrupted by a constant wrapping on my office door. 'I'm busy on the phone; can you come back later please?' My voice must have conveyed the frustration I was experiencing because the sound of meandering footsteps finally faded away. I was unconsciously tapping my foot in time to a beguiling piece of modern jazz swirling around in my head when a voice interrupted.

'I've found her. Hold on, she's coming, she's almost here.' Before I had time to thank the excited and helpful Pat Norman she was gone. Then a voice that I half recognised began to speak. 'Hello, is the Dennis I danced with on

Saturday?' It was her, Patricia Norman, a.k.a Gill Norman, and what's more she remembered me. 'Yes it is,' I replied. 'I was beginning to think you were being evasive when you told me where you worked.' I stopped to consider the situation. 'It's a bit confusing having another Pat Norman in the same salon, isn't it?' I heard some girly giggling before she answered. 'Well it was a bit confusing when I was given a new name, but I've got used to it now. I should have thought of it when I introduced myself. Look, I don't want to be difficult, but I have a client waiting and I'll be in big trouble if she's not attended to. Why don't you call me at home this evening?' She gave me the phone number and rang off. I smiled to myself, delighted that the next step in the dating process was within reach.

However, I was not privy to the fact that Patricia already had a steady boyfriend and, what's more, he was the apple of her father's eye!

CHAPTER NINE

We have never had the benefit of a telephone in my parent's apartment, which wasn't unusual because nine out of ten homes in the late fifties (1950's that is) were in the same position. Putting food on the table took precedent over extravagances such as telephones, so I had to walk to the nearest public telephone box situated about fifty yards from the apartment. There was a middle-aged woman slouching in the phone box when I arrived. She had the phone rammed up against her right ear and was leaning against the door in a don't-disturb-me-or-you're-in-big-trouble attitude that spoke volumes. She glanced briefly at me and then quickly reverted to her original position, words pouring out of her mouth like Niagara in full flood. After some minutes I dared a light tap on the door. She turned around, glared at me, and shifted her position so that her back was blocking my view of the interior. I was growing increasingly annoyed so I took hold of the handle and gently eased the door partly open. I spoke through the gap.

'I need to speak to someone urgently. Are you going to be long?'

'Close the door,' she hissed. 'I can be as long as I like. If I was you I'd go to another phone box.'

It is at times like this when one realises how difficult some people can be. The next phone box was at least a quarter of a mile distant. In any case, I had come to regard this particular phone box as mine, because of its close proximity and the dozens of times I have used it. Now here was someone telling me to get lost and I didn't like it.

'All I need is five minutes on the phone and then you can have it back and use it for as long as you like.' I tried my best to sound persuasively calm and I must have succeeded because she spoke a final few words into the phone and slammed down the receiver. 'Lucky for you I'm in a good mood,' she said stepping through the now opened door. 'It's all yours.'

I thanked her and stepped into the phone box. I had Patricia's phone number embedded in my memory and dialled it. A gruff male voice answered.

'Can I speak to Patricia please?'

'Who wants to speak to her?'

'Dennis.'

'Dennis? I don't know you do I?'

'No you don't but then I don't know you either.'

'I'm her father, that's who I am.'

I knew I had made a grave mistake. His voice had become even more gruff and I feared he was about to put the phone down, but then I heard a female voice in the background. She was asking who was on the phone.

'It's someone called Dennis. He wants to talk to you.'

I could hear muttering as the receiver was handed over.

'Hello Dennis,' Patricia's voice was subdued. 'Nice of you to call. How are you?'

'I'm well. Just hoping I haven't upset your dad.'

'Dad's always crotchety when he answers the phone, so no change there.'

'I hope I get the opportunity to meet him. What does he do for a living?'

'He's with a printing company called Twinlock; been with then for as long as I can remember. He has worked his way up the promotion ladder and is in line for Managing Director when the present MD retires in a year's time. I hope it works out for him because he works all hours, including weekends.'

Now I knew why he sounded gruff: obviously he works too hard and it detrimentally colours his personality. I'll have to choose my words carefully when, if, I next speak to him. I decided to change the subject.

'So Patricia, after you've finished work one evening, would you like to go to the cinema?' Receiving an affirmative nod, I carried on. 'Do you know the Hippodrome in Shaftesbury Avenue? There's a Norman Wisdom film, which is supposed to be funny. What do you think?'

'Yes, it sounds fine. I like Norman Wisdom; he reminds me of my Uncle Vic.'

Notwithstanding a positive answer or her Uncle Vic, I could sense she was giving some thought to the date.

'Can we make it tomorrow evening because that's the only one I get to finish on time? Every other evening I'm teaching apprentices how to become hairdressers.'

'Hmm, sounds as if you are like your dad; working all hours; it must run in the family.'

'Yes that's true. Mum works really hard but there is one exception; my older sister, she's known by her Aunt Marje as Princess because she doesn't lift a finger to help at home, and she's probably the same at work. She's a secretary in London, nine to five, long lunch breaks, every weekend off. Doesn't know she's born. But enough of that, I'll see you outside the cinema on Tuesday. What time?'

'Make it six o'clock and we'll have time for a coffee before the film starts.'

We said our goodbyes. I was really happy. Although tomorrow seemed a long way off, I knew it was going to be worth the wait.

I can't recall much about the film or whether it was funny. What I do recall, however, is sitting in the back row of the circle and, after a while, putting an arm around Patricia's shoulder. She looked at me and whispered a chastening, 'Please don't do that.' She obviously thought I was being too forward on a first date so, as a means of reconciliation, I bought two chocolate ice creams during the interval one of which she accepted with a forgiving smile. It was clearly evident I would have to be careful not to rush things otherwise there would be no future for us.

We left the cinema, crossed the road, and jumped on a bus to Charing Cross railway station. Patricia's train to Beckenham was leaving on schedule in ten minutes; my train to Charlton was not due to leave for another twenty minutes so we had time to meander down the busy platform looking for a window seat from where Patricia could wave farewell as her train departed.

'Call me tomorrow, at home,' she mouthed silently from behind the window. A series of nods and a wave from me indicated my understanding. The train slid noisily away and left me staring at its rear before it disappeared round a bend into the murky darkness.

Our first date was over and I was left wondering, uncertain. Had it been a success? Well, she asked me to call her tomorrow, so that has to be a plus point…..I think, I hope.

CHAPTER TEN

It certainly was worth the wait. Over the next eighteen months the bond between Patricia and yours truly grew stronger and we eventually married on July 8, 1961. I was twenty-six, Patricia a month short of twenty years of age. That chance meeting at The Lyceum Ballroom had led inexorably to the altar of St. John's Church in Penge, South East-London.

The wedding ceremony was magical. Patricia looked absolutely stunning in her white bridal gown, accompanied as she was by her four bridesmaids dressed in pink. In addition to Patricia's family and friends were my three brothers, their wives, several of my long term friends and some colleagues from UPI. One uninvited guest was standing alone outside the waist high church wall. It was the apple of Patricia's dad's eye, her ex-boyfriend Roy. I didn't see him but Patricia did, although she didn't mention it until some months later.

The wedding ceremony affected me in unexpected and inexplicable ways. I emanated nervousness, elation, joy and other emotions I had never previously experienced. As we left the church, as man and wife, the rain, which had been forecast, and which we had prayed would not come to pass, began to fall a trifle reluctantly, as if not wishing to spoil the happy occasion. The official photographer took up her position in front of the main entrance to the church, apparently ignoring the splattering wetness. She indicated where we were to stand, accompanied by the bridesmaids, our respective mothers and fathers and my best man, my dear brother Fred.

The wedding reception was a huge success due, totally, unquestioningly, to Patricia's parents. So much effort, so much planning, so much expense, had been lavished upon it that I felt humbled by their generosity. Patricia had discarded her bridal gown and was now wearing a lovely two-piece orange coloured going-away suit, specially created as a wedding present by her friend Daphne, who was a deft hand in the art of tailoring and design.

It was almost seven p.m. and everyone appeared to be enjoying themselves; eating, chatting, laughing, dancing, singing, and basking in the warmth of the occasion. I whispered to Patricia, who was sitting next to me, while talking non-stop to one of the bridesmaids, her best friend Barbara.

"Sorry to interrupt, we have to be leaving soon, our plane takes off at 10 o'clock and we have to get to the airport. I think I should make an announcement.' She agreed. I stood up and let everyone know that our honeymoon was about to commence, and we had to leave promptly. Cheering all round. We had arranged for Barbara and her boyfriend Roger to take us to Gatwick airport, where we would board an aeroplane for Palma the capital city of Mallorca. My dream to marry Patricia was now a reality and I knew, unequivocally, I now had a partner for life.

We honeymooned at the Mar y Vent Hotel, in the village of Banyalbufar situated on the northwest coast of the Balearic island of Mallorca. It was around three o'clock in the morning when the taxi dropped us off at the hotel. We entered the reception area, signed in and were allocated a room on the second floor. We were each handed a lighted candle and escorted to our room. (At breakfast the following morning we were informed that the generator supplying electricity to the village was switched off every midnight; hence the need for candles!) Tired beyond anything we had ever experienced, we fell into a dreamless sleep and were rudely awoken by bright sunlight entering uninvited into our room between gaps in the curtains.

The view from the window of our room was spectacular; terrace upon terrace of vibrantly green vineyards spiralling down towards the blue Mediterranean; the early morning sun sparkling and glittering on its surface in a show of welcome to an excited pair of newly-weds. We showered, dressed, and walked down the winding staircase to the dining room where we were greeted by the owners, Antonio and Juanita Vives. Big Spanish smiles accompanied firm Spanish handshakes. We were led to a table on the imposing terrace overlooking the same view we had witnessed from our bedroom. From the terrace it looked even more beautiful. We sat down at a table and a young, male, waiter appeared. He handed us a menu and greeted us in charming, broken, English. We both chose the same; scrambled eggs, toast, croissants, orange juice and marmalade followed later by aromatic coffee. Our first meal together as a married couple was an occasion I remember as clearly today as if it had happened only yesterday.

CHAPTER ELEVEN

Our first home was a rented, cramped, one bedroom flat in Shortlands, a couple of miles from the town of Bromley in the county of Kent. Despite its many shortcomings, we loved it. From our first floor windows we could see the south facing garden. Mainly laid to lawn, it was enclosed by immaculately trimmed, ten feet high, beech hedges. In the centre of the lawn was an ancient oak tree, its leafy branches stretching out and upwards as if seeking to touch the fluffy white clouds floating in the pale blue sky. A rope swing was attached to the lowest, sturdy, branch; clear evidence that a child or children were present in the converted property. The sitting/dining room was just large enough, with some judicious placement, to house our recently purchased furniture; a round wooden table and four matching chairs, a three-seater, dark blue, couch and a small refrigerator. The kitchen was so small that only one person could safely function within it. It had an ancient gas oven, a small, metal sink and two small cupboards above to house our crockery and food.

Finding a suitable spot for the refrigerator was a challenge that Patricia's cousin Terry cheerfully undertook. He cut off the bottom half of the door fronting the entrance hall storage cupboard and successfully manoeuvred the refrigerator into place. What our landlord would make of such a violation we declined to consider; such was our satisfaction at finding a home where we could settle down and be happy. The bedroom was large enough to take our new double bed. Fortunately built-in wardrobes and a sturdy chest of drawers saved us the expense of buying such necessities. The oak-tree-dominated garden was a calming sight from the bedroom's double window while the only sound was that of birds constantly chirping as they competed for space among the tree's branches. It appeared as if we had acquired a haven of peace for an annual rental of £300.

We spent three very happy years at the flat before we embarked on a mission to buy our own home. House buying back in the early 1960's was just beginning to be favoured over renting. Problem was, I was only earning £1,500 a year. However, properties were relatively inexpensive so we grabbed the bull by its horns and took out a 90% mortgage on a new, very unique, bungalow in Tunbridge Wells priced at £4,850 pounds! Imagine that when compared with today's soaring prices. The same bungalow would, without any shadow of doubt, realise an asking price of at least £485,000 today.

The bungalow was conveniently situated for almost everything we needed. Within walking distance was the best butcher's shop in Tunbridge Wells. It was so popular that, whenever we went to buy something, there was always a queue. The railway station, from where I commuted to London five days a week, was a fifteen minute walk down a series of steep, winding hills. The problem was, it was a steep winding hill to struggle up after a long day at work. Sometimes Patricia would drive down and pick me up in our first car, a Sunbeam Alpine sports car which Terry, Patricia's cousin (he who cut the door in half in our flat) sold to us at a large discount. We learned the reason why he was so generous when a policeman rapped on the door of the bungalow after a few weeks and asked to see the car's log book. It transpired that our car was, in fact, the front and the back of two damaged Sunbeam Alpines which had been expertly welded together at Terry's garage in South London. As far as I can recall no action was taken against Terry. But it taught us a very valuable lesson; if something looks too good to be true, it very likely isn't. Whatever, the car never let us down and we are still close friends with Terry who, incidentally, ended up owning a large farm on the outskirts of Surrey where he continued to expand his business activities. A huge garage on the farm has become home to a dazzling array of classic cars, and not one of them was the result of Terry's expertise at welding!

CHAPTER TWELVE

Our first child, Scott, was born on July 1, 1967, three years after we settled into our much loved bungalow. His birth had been traumatic but he was an unexpected blessing since we had been informed by a family doctor, prior to our marriage, that the likelihood of Patricia having children was extremely low. We proved the doctor wrong and the result was a chubby faced boy who always appeared to be happy and content, if his constant smiling was anything to go by that is. Five years later, on May 24, 1972, our second son, Christian, was born. Birthing-wise he was the opposite of his brother in that he entered the world with no fuss, without the week-long, prolonged trauma which accompanied his brother's birth, and his beaming smile lit our lives as does the most sparkling of candelabras.

Despite my need to commute by train each workday to UPI's office in London's Bouverie Street, life was good. I was working hard at expanding the company's client base throughout Europe, Africa and the Middle East. This involved much travelling but I relished the opportunity to visit countries I had read about in newspapers and travel magazines. Rome was a city I fell in love with during my first visit. It was so different, primarily because of its millennium-long, chequered, history. Even now, fifty-five years after my first visit, I frequently think of Rome and the wonderful sights that so entranced me.

Rome was also where I learned to make Spaghetti Carbonara. I often dined at a restaurant called Il Moro and, after a number of visits, I caught the attention of the proprietor because my order was invariably Spaghetti Carbonara. He was so pleased that I liked Il Moro's version of this popular Italian dish that he took me to the restaurant's kitchen and was shown how it was made. To this day I still make the dish exactly as I was taught by the chef at Il Moro, and it receives plaudits from family and friends whenever it is featured on a menu at home.

Over the next several years I attended business appointments in each and every capital city in Europe plus a special one in the Middle East; Tel Aviv, the uniquely endowed capital city of Israel. The people I encountered there displayed a unique brand of stoicism which, without I believe, has to be the result of the terrible atrocities which have been perpetrated upon the Jewish people over the past two thousand years.

My first visit to Tel Aviv was marred by my catching a stomach bug which had me squirming with pain in my bed at the hotel for three miserable days. The hotel's doctor assured me I was in safe hands and prescribed a variety of pills and medicines, the combination of which eventually resulted in a return to a semblance of good health. The doctor warned me to refrain from eating the local grapes, unless they had been washed thoroughly before consuming. I don't think it was unwashed grapes which caused my stomach to rebel against any incoming food; I think it was a combination of eating unusual foods, drinking water which was not fresh, by UK standards that is, and a susceptibility to anything left out of a refrigerator for far too long.

CHAPTER THIRTEEN

It was in April of 1984, the 28th year of my employment at UPI, that I became increasingly aware the company was in serious financial trouble. The warning signs were cogently evident if only one took the trouble to read them. I was still working hard at expanding the company's business activities but stiff competition from Reuters and Associated Press resulted in existing clients looking to cut their costs by negotiating cheaper deals with our competitors. I had recently been to UPI's headquarters at 220 East 42nd St., New York and noted an invasive air of depression permeating the atmosphere. Apparently an American company, alien to the production of television news, general news, news photos and features, had placed a bid for the company; a company whose sordid business was built upon buying up, for a song, businesses in financial trouble, identifying the portions which could be sold off while ignoring the other portions without any apparent value.

Upon my return to UPI's headquarters in London I was made aware that there was nothing that could be done to save the company I had come to love over the years. Reuters had stepped in and bought the news pictures and television news slices of UPI's business. Some of UPI's journalists and photographers were switched to Reuter's payroll, others were made redundant. It was the saddest time in my life, to see a company whose world-wide reputation had been paramount above all others, now down in the gutter and unable to do anything to find its feet. Later that day I had a meeting with UPI's London based Vice President and was told my job was at an end. Shocking as was this news it could have been worse.

Without knowing how it happened, I had concurrently been head hunted by a company whose business was booming and they wanted me to help make it boom even louder; the company was Henson International Television (HIT) whose owner was the one and only Jim Henson, a man who made the world of film and television laugh uproariously at his unique blend of comic genius.

CHAPTER FOURTEEN

I was interviewed at the Intercontinental Hotel located in London's Park Lane by a newly appointed Vice President of Henson International Television; can't remember his name. Memory starts to erode when one gets to my stage in life. I do recall however, without overly stressing my brain, that he was American. We had a congenial meal and a very encouraging exchange of views which resulted in my accepting the terms being offered; a two year contract at the same annual salary I received at United Press International. I had anticipated a somewhat larger slice of the HIT financial pie but was encouraged by the possibility of an annual bonus if specified fiscal targets were reached and exceeded. My position was to be Managing Director of Henson Enterprises; a new offshoot whose objective was to distribute the company's products into new fields including books, magazines, newspapers, etc. It was an opportunity to show what I could accomplish with the well-established Henson tools in my newly opened workshop, and I was determined to hammer home the opportunity.

The Henson offices were located in a prestigious position just off Leicester Square when my employment commenced; an easy walk back and forth to Charing Cross Station where trains from Tunbridge Wells terminated their daily journeys. Unfortunately (and I should have been informed of this before accepting the position) the company's offices were soon to be relocated to Hampstead, an up market location in the north of London. That's how life goes, is it not? One minute you are sitting pretty, the next you are presented with an unexpected piece of information which changes "sitting pretty" to something far less comfortable. What this meant to me, commuter-wise, was taking an earlier train than usual to London's Charing Cross station, followed by two separate underground trains to Hampstead. My comfort zone was reduced before I had even started my new position as MD of Henson Enterprises. Was this a bad omen or just one of life's eternal twists and turns?

It turned out to be a bad omen, unfortunately. I had signed a two year contract when I joined the Jim Henson organisation but, after only one year, it became obvious I didn't fit into the unique pattern woven by Jim and his staff. It wasn't anything to do with antipathy towards me but rather a way of working with which I was totally unfamiliar. Jim was a great guy and sent me a note to say how pleased he was to have me aboard. The thing which stands out during the initial year was a trip to Australia with several of the Henson staffers. I was provided with a first class return to Sydney with Qantas Airways which, with company approval, I changed for two club class tickets for my wife Patricia and myself. It was a wonderful week but I remain puzzled to this day as to what the visit was about and what was achieved. We met the local Henson representative, Fred Gaffney, a lovely man, an archetypal Aussie who lived life to the full. He arranged for us to go to the Australian Tennis Open where seventeen-year-old Boris Becker was demonstrating his unique talent for the first time on the other side of the world. Even to those with little knowledge of the game, it was obvious that a bright new star was about to change the way tennis would be played in future. His speed around the court, his versatility and his never say die attitude would undoubtedly change the face of world tennis for decades to come.

Another Henson event which remains forever etched in my memory bank was a party at a restaurant in a suburb of Sydney, known locally as The Cross but actually named after London's Kings Cross. All of the Henson employees, plus my wife Patricia, were there and, unforgivably, over the course of the evening I had a little too much to drink. As the party wound down with the approach of midnight, a few of us hopped into a stretched limo for the journey back to our hotel. Horror of horrors, I suddenly realised my wife was not one of the limo's passengers. Where was she? Panic caused my drunken state to melt like an ice cream exposed to the afternoon sun on Sydney's Bondi Beach.

Kings Cross is notorious as a red-light district where its brothels, organised crime and other odious activities are played out on a daily basis. It was not the ideal place for my wife to be left on her own. I decided to get a taxi back to the restaurant and, as I burst through the entrance, the manager confronted me. 'Have you seen my wife?' I asked diffidently. 'I thought she was with me in the limo but she wasn't and now I don't know where she is.'

The manager shook his head. 'This is a very dangerous district for anyone, never mind a lovely young woman such as your wife……'

'I know, I know,' I replied with a large dose of chagrin. 'But do you have any idea where she is?'

The manager glowered before answering in a tone that had me shaking like a schoolboy waiting outside his headmaster's office expecting a few strokes of the cane.

'Yes, I know exactly where she is. I asked one of my waitresses to call a cab and accompany your wife to your hotel. The waitress is now back and Patricia, your wife, is safe and sound and no doubt waiting to tear your heart out, because that's what my wife would do if I treated her the way you treated your wife.'

I started to make an excuse but was abruptly silenced by the rigid palm of the manager's hand being raised in the front of my anguished face. 'You were drunk and you are extremely lucky I didn't call the police. Now please leave and I trust your wife will apply appropriate retribution upon her erring husband.'

I knocked on the door of our room in the hotel and, after several agonising seconds, Patricia opened it. Her face was devoid of expression and her body language left me in no doubt that I was most certainly not the flavour of the month.

'Can I come in please?' My quivering voice betrayed utmost anxiety.

Patricia stepped aside and allowed me to pass. She shut the door and followed me. I could feel her gaze burning the back of my head as if she had honed it on a leather strap. It was now past midnight and I was thinking of the comfortable bed we had shared the past several days. It was not to be.

'You can sleep on the couch tonight,' hissed Patricia tossing me a pillow and blanket. 'I have never been so humiliated in my life. If it wasn't for the manager and his waitress I would probably have ended up getting raped or worse.'

With that she turned around and went back to the bedroom, closing the door with dramatic finality. I stripped, except for my underpants, and lay down on the much-too-short couch, nestling my head on the pillow and drawing the thin blanket up around my shoulders.

The following morning, after a quiet breakfast, Patricia appeared to have forgiven me. We strolled, hand in hand, along the bustling streets leading to Sydney Harbour, and stood, open-mouthed, gaping at the Sydney Opera House which was ostensibly floating in the sparkling blue waters of the harbour. The Opera House looks like a ship with several sails unfurled, a beautiful sight to satisfy the most discerning of people.

'We must go there before we leave Australia,' said Patricia, still overwhelmed by the hypnotic aura we were witnessing. 'Can we do that?'

As of this moment I would have done anything she asked for, such was my relief at having regained the love of Patricia, my lovely wife.

'Of course my love, just as soon as we know how long we are here for and when we have some free time. What I'd really like to do however is to change our flights home and make a stop at Bali for a few days. How does that sound?'

Patricia looked stunned. 'Are you sure we could do that without causing problems at work? Everything seems so relaxed, I can't really believe a company would spend so much on a visit which appears to have produced nothing tangible.'

I nodded my understanding and smiled. 'There's no harm in trying is there?' After an amiable discussion I received approval and two days later we were on an Indonesian airliner heading for Bali. Which was great but I still failed to understand how a company could spend so much money without receiving something in return.

Bali was a big disappointment. Our rickety taxi passed innumerable roadside paddy fields being tended by weary-looking women, up to their knees in brackish-looking water, before arriving at our hotel. Which appeared fine on the surface except for the fact that everywhere you looked, everything you touched, was constantly damp; so much so that it was impossible to see through the windows into the near beyond. We only stayed three days and then flew back to London. Being home was a blessed relief after a succession of odd, strange events, beginning with those in Australia and ending with the mysteries experienced in Indonesia. On reflection perhaps it was Patricia and I who were the oddities in this series of unusual events? Whatever, my task now was to develop my relationship with colleagues at Henson Enterprises and expand my business activities. I had twenty-eight years of solid experience at United Press International. Surely I could utilise that experience to drive my particular responsibilities of the Henson business forward? I was more than willing to give it a try.

CHAPTER FIFTEEN

The most annoying thing about getting to the Henson offices in Hampstead was the underground trains which, at times, were delayed and resulted in my being late for company meetings. I always left my home in Tunbridge Wells with what I considered included was plenty of time to spare. Not so. Those damned underground trains were invariably late and, consequently, I was embarrassed on several occasions, one of which involved the current CEO, the man who hired me after our meeting at The Intercontinental Hotel some months ago. I tried to explain my late arrival but he ignored me and carried on with the staff meeting as if I was not there.

I was totally frustrated and requested a meeting to vent my feelings. I told the CEO I was not prepared to accept his admonitions and wished to leave the company as soon as possible. We discussed the situation and eventually, to my delight and benefit, we agreed I should leave immediately. Compensation for the residue of my two year agreement would be in the post today. Consequently, I was out of work but looking forward to a refreshing break before seeking new employment. Where would that be was the big question?

CHAPTER SIXTEEN

I cannot recall, neither can I attempt to determine, exactly how long I was out of work between leaving Henson and joining CNN International. How I managed to first, find a position that suited my rather altruistic nature, and second, to actually land a job that offered a huge variety of challenges. Allow me to explain. CNN was, prior to its expansion as a world-wide 24 hours-a-day news organisation, USA based and that was it.

It was Ted Turner who took the decision to initiate and create a world-wide version of the very popular programme and it certainly presented me with an opportunity to move forward after the disastrous year spent with Jim Henson's organisation. I cannot recall how or where I saw the advert for a position at CNN International but I was pleased to have landed a position which, undoubtedly, would stretch my abilities to the utmost. The first CNN International office was located in a grimy backstreet in London where the staff consisted of me, plus three more men. Two were American and the third was English. Our task was to promote CNN International to as wide an audience as possible throughout Europe and the Middle East. We started in a very low key way by approaching cable systems in the United Kingdom to determine whether there may be interest in making CNN International available at a very low cost per customer. This turned out to be fruitless and so we changed tactics. Carry the programme, free of charge, and we would approach advertisers who would pay an appropriate fee relative to the number of viewers being reached. This also landed on deaf ears. To be effective an advertiser needs a wide, distinct, audience which reacts to the messages being transmitted. The UK CNN International cable audience most definitely did not fit this profile. So we sat down and, after much argument, decided what to do next. Cable systems throughout Europe were already well established and very successful. It made good sense, therefore, to concentrate on this existing market which undoubtedly would produce tangible rewards in the future.

Included in the 24-hours-a-day programming was a 15 minute piece entitled CNN Newsroom. Transmitted Monday through Friday, it was proving to be very popular in European schools where children, eager to improve their English, had access to something much more interesting than their books.

So, we now had something tangible to build upon. The result, after months of success and failure, was something with which we had good reason to be extremely proud.

+ + +

The following six years were a toxic mix of toil and disappointment which nonetheless, resulted in CNN International finally becoming available to 200 million households and hotel rooms in 200 countries. Ted Turner at this stage must have been delighted because he and his then wife, the actress Jane Fonda, visited the new London office of CNN International to congratulate those who had been instrumental in its success. I recall standing next to Ms. Fonda as Ted addressed the assembled staff. The beam on his craggy features remained throughout the meeting – a testament to his delight at a venture that looked, at times, to be doomed to failure. He spoke profusely about the dedication and perseverance of his employees when all appeared to be heading in the wrong direction. Now the challenge was to generate advertising income. But that is another story yet to be unfolded.

CHAPTER SEVENTEEN

I was employed at CNN International for ten years, ending my tenure as Vice President, Corporate Development. When the company was taken over by Time Warner things, for me and my long term colleagues, took a turn for the worse. Time Warner rushed to bring in their own staff and turfed out those, including me, who had worked so assiduously to achieve success over the past ten years. I was now 60 years of age and out of work. Why would any company hire someone of my age?

Fortunately, I had some good contacts at the BBC and although I was hired I knew it was only for a short term. BBC World and BBC Prime were two programmes about to be launched and it was the responsibility of a number of colleagues, including yours truly, to ensure the programmes were viewed as widely as possible.

If this sounds similar to the problems encountered with the launch of CNN International, I would have to agree. It was akin to starting all over again.

CHAPTER EIGHTEEN

I decided it is no use worrying about what might be because there are so many unforeseen events occurring outside of one's control. Rather I have decided to concentrate on the positive, while ignoring anything negative. I will only focus on things which, aligned to a positive attitude, will result in a beneficial outcome. In other words, I am now through with anything that causes grief and heartache. I am a new me. Onwards and upwards is my motto and nothing will be allowed to stop me climbing to the zenith. I now realise that the adoption of positive thinking kicks negativity right where it should be, down there in the gutter. Consequently, from now on, nothing will be allowed to stand in the way of a future bright with promise. There, I've said it, and now it's up to me to ensure my decisions are enacted.

CHAPTER NINETEEN

Five days later, I received a call from Hector Elizalde. We discussed, in minute detail, what kind of person Don King was looking for. Did I have all of the attributes necessary to satisfy a man whose world-wide boxing business accumulated income at a level which would give cause for a billionaire to boggle? Did I want to give up everything I had in the UK and migrate to sun-drenched Florida where an uncertain future beckoned? The decision became clear when I looked at the situation from an outsider's point of view. This told me, unequivocally, that my wife and I should accept the offer of an all-expenses-paid trip to Florida which would provide an opportunity to see what, where and how, Don King's organisation was run.

It wasn't very convincing, the visit to view DK's organisation that is. A scruffy set of offices where, we were told, beware of parking our car out back because of a number of recurring car thefts. We were shown around the offices by a woman named Celia who appeared to have a dominating influence over the staff and over DK himself which surprised me. Our unpretentious hotel was located several miles away in a northerly direction but, at least, the tortuous drive presented the opportunity for us to have a serious chat about our situation. To say we were unconvinced about my working for Don King would be putting it mildly. In fact we both thought a swift return to the UK would be our best bet.

'Let's give it a few days,' proposed my wife after thoughtful consideration. 'First impressions are sometimes the wrong ones.'

She was right of course. We had to determine what the future held for us and the only way to do that was for me to become involved in DK's every-day business life. So I knuckled down and utilised my hard earned skills to see how I could immerse myself into something which, at the present moment, I knew less about than one particular employee named Andy, a young man whose task was to prepare and hand out drinks and sandwiches! He earned my respect in so doing because he was always courteous and smiling. The other employees, Glenda, Janet, Maria, Louisa and Doris were all working their butts off but appeared to resent my presence if sly, whispered, back-of-the-hand, comments were any indication. On the contrary my good friend, Raphael, the man responsible for ringside satellite broadcasts, gave me a black Ralph Lauren polo shirt which I still have and treasure. It's strange how some of the earliest incidents in life remain at the back of one's mind while others, more current, are filtered away, never to see the light of day.

The situation changed for the better, when it was made known to DK's employees, that the new corporate offices are now officially open at 501, Fairway Drive, Deerfield Beach, Florida. This was exciting news although it meant, for some employees, a long drive from their homes located close to the crime ridden, poverty stricken, down town office. For the two of us, however, it was good news because the apartment we rented at San Marco was only a ten minute drive from DK's new office. At long last, our luck was changing and we could start to enjoy life. I surprised my wife after a month or so by part exchanging her aging Suzuki Swift for a brand new Honda Civic. She was absolutely delighted and we celebrated its arrival by using it to drive to our favourite restaurant, Romano's Macaroni Grill. The food was always excellent and, after finishing our meal, I used the pencils provided to draw the faces of first, my wife, and then other patrons, on the white surface of the paper-covered tables. One dear friend, Milly, was so impressed with my artistic ability that she took the drawing home and had it framed.

CHAPTER TWENTY

I remained unable to convince the five staff who reported to me that I was an asset who was determined to create a wide-ranging, working environment, where opinions were taken into account and acted upon, if deemed appropriate. My PA, Louisa, eventually became a friend who dropped her frosty manner and began accepting the value of some of my directives. DK's Senior Vice President, Cecelia, a woman who worked without pause, seven days a week, also appeared to be warming towards me. Perhaps due to a system I created which underlined exactly where we had to concentrate in order to maximise income from our world-wide list of clients. I introduced twice-a-week staff meetings where I handed out details of our sales progress and what needed to be done to ensure a successful conclusion.

Clients could choose between receiving live satellite transmission of a boxing programme or delayed rights, which meant forwarding video tape recordings; a lengthy and onerous task.

Cecelia however, was loath to change her ways. She insisted we forward our client's contracts, page by page, by means of a teleprinter which, to put it mildly, was a laborious chore. We then had to wait until the client responded. Tedium was cogently evident throughout the office as testified by the sound of muffled yawns. One of my five staff, Louisa, always left exactly at five pm because she had a young family to attend to, and, what is more, she had a long drive back to her home close to the old DK office. I quite understood Louisa's problem but Cecelia could only shake her head: her dark brown eyes conveying a modicum of emotion.

I looked at her, shaking my head in disbelief.

'I know you're a workaholic.' I said 'But the point is that some of us have a life outside of Don King Productions. We don't live to work, but work to live.'

Cecelia now had another object to aim her barbs at, poor little me.

'I think you should pick your words with great care,' she said. 'As Senior Vice President I have seniority over you and, if you cannot accept that, then we have a problem.'

I decided enough was enough.

'Let's get back to work,' I said. 'Otherwise we'll forget what we are supposed to be doing.'

This was the day when Cecelia and I had to decide my future role with Don King Productions. I couldn't work with a harness hanging around my neck so, to pen a phrase; I took the bull by the horns.

'It's Patricia's birthday today. Why don't you join us at our apartment this evening for a celebratory meal?'

Cecelia's acceptance offered a degree of solace to a tricky situation.

CHAPTER TWENTY-ONE

I decided the time had arrived to utilise to my own advantage the expertise gained from my employment at UPI, Henson Enterprises and CNN International. The task confronting me was simple; to somehow override Cecelia's objections.

I knew what had to be done but I also had to be certain that my proposal would prevail against any objections, especially from Cecelia.

Don King, I was sure, would welcome the opportunity to visit the Princedom of Monaco, as it is so quaintly known. Prince Albert was on the throne and welcomed the opening of Sportel, since people attending the event spend vast sums of money on hotels, the gaming casino and in the gaudy pubs where hard liquor is consumed without a thought for the morrow.

The Prince's interest in events occurring within his Princedom never wavers. Hence the four days of Sportel is at the top of his agenda and he is aware that it is, without a shadow of doubt, the most influential business venue for the global sports media industry. Buyers from around the world attend to acquire enough sporting programmes to satisfy their viewers for the coming year. Sellers, on the other hand, have cause to thank Sportel for the opportunity to top up their bank accounts!

Sellers rent marquees above which their company logos are displayed. This presents to opportunity to speak to buyers in a relaxed atmosphere, resulting in some buyers becoming friends.

Sportel therefore is my trump card and leaves Cecelia with a conundrum; will she seize the opportunity or reject it?

In life one can never be sure of anything. It was Robbie Burns who wrote, *The Best Laid Plans of Mice and Men oft go astray.* So, bearing that in mind, I had move carefully, thus ensuring Cecelia will embrace my plan to go to Monaco and see, first hand, what Sportel has to offer. I had another trump card to play. As soon as Cecelia says she'll go to Monaco I will telephone my PA back in Florida, and ask her to suggest Don King joins us. I trust he will because, like all celebrities, he loves to be recognised by adoring fans. He could also be introduced to another celebrity, Prince Albert! Now, who could resist that?

My ruse worked to perfection. Don King and Cecelia were set to fly to Nice airport (Monaco doesn't have one) tomorrow. I will go to the airport to meet them and transport them to the hotel where they will stay during the four days of Sportel. If I was able to clap myself on the back, I would do so, but my arms aren't long enough.

I am absolutely delighted that things are going my way. So much so that I might have a couple of beers at the hotel bar before I retire to my bed.

The telephone rang a minute or so after I pulled the bedclothes around my neck. I snatched at the receiver and recognised my PA's excited voice.

"We are coming to Monaco with DK and Cecelia, all five of us!"

"What do you mean all five of you?"

"I mean me, Miranda, Jennie, Louisa and Kathy. We're all on the same flight. You will meet us won't you?"

I stopped to gather my breath, after it had been taken away by the unexpected news. "Yes, of course I'll meet you,' I gasped. 'I'll have to hire a limo, but Don can pick up the tab."

'I'm sure he will," said Alexis. "Goodbye for now. See you tomorrow."

I dreamt the dreams of a tormented soul and woke in the morning, my brain overflowing like a dam after a week of incessant rain.

My plans had come to fruition, albeit not as originally conceived.

Don King and Cecelia were first to appear at arrivals gate. Following them were Miranda, Alexis, Jennie and Kathy, their delighted smiles made my wait worthwhile. Don and Cecelia, however, looked as if a pungent smell had suffused their noses.

I waved to catch their attention. Don approached me and stuck out a plump hand which I shook warmly. Cecelia merely nodded at me and climbed into the limo. Don, ever the gentleman, held the rear door open and motioned for his employees to sit on the rear seats.

During the drive to the hotel there was some back of the hand whispering, which ceased immediately when

Cecelia waved an authoritative hand. Don looked ahead, taking in the magnificent view as the road curled around a steep headland which overlooked the sparkling, blue, Mediterranean far below. It was evident that Don was impressed and I silently congratulated myself upon realising I had secured another link in my plan for DK, Cecelia and his employees to attend Sportel.

Upon arrival in Monaco I pulled up at the Meridien Beach Hotel, expecting the occupants of the limo to alight and make their way towards the hotel entrance. Six of us alighted, but Don and Cecelia remained seated in the limo.

"Don and I are staying at The Hermitage," said Cecilia. "We will see you all evening for dinner at the Meridien Beach, where we will inform you where our company stand is located and what must be done to make it attractive so that it stands out from the other competitors."

Without any more ado Cecelia tapped me on the shoulder and said, "The Hermitage hotel please." I shook my head in disbelief and prayed Cecelia had seen my silent response.

The company stand was positioned close to the entrance of the huge hall. It was an ideal location for sellers and buyers. I was standing adjacent to the stand when DK saw me. He patted me on the back.

"Well done.' he said, a wide grin on his face. "The stand looks great." He pointed to the sign DON KING PRODUCTIONS which was printed in red on a canopy stretched across the top of the stand.

Of Cecelia there was no sign. Alexis, Miranda, Jennie, Louisa and Kathy, broad smiles on their excited faces, approached the stand. Don greeted them warmly, as does a proud father to his five children.

Fronting the stand were ropes arranged like those surrounding a boxing ring. My idea, I have to say. They underlined the fact that DON KING PRODUCTIONS was foremost in the boxing business. Pinned up around the interior of the stand were large, coloured, photographs of Mike Tyson and Evander Holyfield. A television was running recordings of recent fights promoted by DK. The stand was, without doubt, the most compelling as testified by the excited crowd milling around outside.

I reached into a drawer where I found the leaflets I had left there the previous evening. The leaflets carried a photograph of DK plus an invitation to visit his stand, which offered the opportunity to speak to (and be photographed beside) the world's leading boxing promoter.

I handed a bunch of leaflets to Miranda, Alexis, Jennie, Louisa and Kathy. "Take these and give them to as many people as you can. Once you've done that, come back and help because there will be absolute chaos."

CHAPTER TWENTY-TWO

The DK stand was surrounded by frantic buyers, clamoring to secure rights to forthcoming fight programs. A representative from SKY Broadcasting, a company whose sports programs reach thousands of subscribers throughout Europe, was happy to have secured rights to DK's fight programs for the coming year. A German, speaking guttural English, was also intent upon securing rights for his company. He closed a deal at enormous cost and appeared to be delighted at his success.

DK was happy to fulfill his part of the bargain by placing an arm around the shoulders of delighted buyers while being photographed. He was chatting, smiling and touching those who were eager to be close to the most renowned celebrity in the world of boxing.

Of Cecelia, however, there was no sign. I turned to speak to Miranda.

"Do you know where Cecelia is?"

She shrugged her shoulders. "She rang me this morning. Said she's not feeling well, something about a cold brewing. So she's probably still in bed."

"Oh well," I said. "I'll go and see her later to see if she's any better."

I walked to the Hermitage hotel and headed for the elevator. I knew the floor and the room where Cecelia was resting. Standing in the corridor leading to her room was a woman cleaner. She looked up as I approached.

"Puis je vous aidez?" she said. The French I learned at school came to the fore and I replied confidently.

"Merci beaucoup mais il ne faut pas."

I knocked on Cecelia's door.

'Who is it?" Her voice sounded as if she was suffering from a bad bout of influenza.

"It's David. I've come to see how you are feeling."

I heard the rustling of bedclothes and the brush of feet on the carpeted floor. The door opened to reveal Cecelia wearing a dressing gown.

"Come in," she said and shuffled back to her bed and climbed in.

I waited until she flopped back on the pillow.

"So, are you feeling any better?" I asked, sitting down on a chair by the side of the bed.

"I feel as if I am about to die," she croaked. "But don't call the funeral parlour until I give the word."

She managed a wry smile. I reciprocated. We chatted about how things were at the DK stand and she looked pleased. An hour passed and I looked at my watch,

"I must get back. Things are happening so fast at Sportel and I must go and help."

I hadn't noticed but Cecelia had fallen fast asleep. I stood up and left as quietly as I was able and headed back to Sportel.

There was no doubt that the DK stand was attracting the most attention. The television in the booth was showing recordings of the Thrilla in Manila and the Rumble in the Jungle, two of the most brutal fights in the history of boxing. The recordings were being snapped up by excited buyers for a reason way beyond my comprehension. Okay, they were great fights but to me boxing should not descend to the depths of degradation. The referee should step in and stop a contest if he sees that one of the contestants is close to being punched into unconsciousness. Forget the baying crowd seeking yet more blood-letting and instead concentrate on the unfortunate boxer who may not recover from his injuries. A case in point was Cassius Clay (now Mohammed Ali) whose boxing-ring injuries resulted in him becoming a pitiful figure. Now, aged 79, he emanates vocal stutters and trembling hands, a result of Parkinson's syndrome. He is remembered for his "Float like a Butterfly, Sting like a bee" phrase which typified his fighting style.

The four days of Sportel were over and all concerned declared it a huge success. Don and Cecelia (now recovered from her nasty cold) left for the airport at Nice and boarded the plane to Miami. Miranda, Alexis, Jennie, Louise and Kathy and I were not due to fly until tomorrow so we had time to stroll around the Principality of Monaco, stopping to buy presents for our families back home and eating at tiny restaurants where the waiters spoke only French. It was a memorable experience and something that would remain as a treasured memory for the rest of our lives.

EPILOGUE

After a flight of over ten hours, plus a time change, all eight of us including DK and Cecelia, were ready to crawl into bed and sleep as long as necessary to recover from what had been an arduous ordeal.

After two days we were back at the DK office. Everyone who attended Sportel was seated around a huge desk located adjacent to DK's private office. The meeting was convened to discuss all relevant aspects of the visit to Sportel.

Cecelia was seated in a high-backed chair at the end of the table. She placed a wad of paper on the desk and picked up the adjacent phone.

"Don," she said quietly. "We are ready for you."

She put the phone back and tapped rhythmically on the desk with two fingers. I found it annoying and, by the look on Alexis's face, so did she because she raised her eyes to look at the ceiling above her.

The door to DK's office opened and he walked along the side of the desk until he reached a high-backed chair.

He sat down and acknowledged each person with a nod of his head.

'Okay Cecelia, please open the meeting," he said brusquely.

Cecelia handed copies from the wad of paper in front of her and gave them to Louisa who stood up and circled the desk giving a copy to everyone, including DK who merely glanced at it before setting it aside.

Cecelia waited for several seconds before commencing.

"The paper is a record of the most important things that occurred at Sportel. Please read it and let me have your comments tomorrow because it will help determine whether we attend Sportel America in Miami."

She looked around and noticed the surprise on our faces. She smiled before speaking again.

"I have been informed that, because Sportel Monaco is always hugely successful, a similar version will open in Miami next year! What that means, of course, is we will not have to suffer from jet lag or any of the other problems we experienced when flying to Monaco."

Nodding heads from those seated around the table indicated agreement.

"The income accumulated at Sportel Monaco will now be duplicated by buyers attending Sportel Miami. In the not too distant future Sportel will extend to many more countries throughout the world. Don King Productions will attend if deemed appropriate."

This novel ends with a reminder of Hector Elizalde's words: "If Don King Comes Calling, you would be wise to open the door."

.

Printed in Great Britain
by Amazon